Shared Vision

BUILDING TEAM SUCCESS IN HIGHLY COMPETITIVE ENVIRONMENTS

Dr. Danny Powell

Dr. Jon Metz

Authors:

Dr. Danny Powell

Dr. Jon Metz

Edited by:

Linda Lightbourne

Cover Design & Layout:

Dr. Jon Metz

Copyright © 2020 by Danny M. Powell and Jon D. Metz

Publisher:

Danny M. Powell and Jon D. Metz

ISBN: 978-0-578-77480-0

Shared Vision: Building Team Success in Highly Competitive Environments is available in print softcover on Amazon. The E-book can be purchased and downloaded on Kindle. Printed in the United States of America by KDP, an Amazon company.

Contents

Acknowledgments

My work in this book is dedicated to the leaders in my life. First of all to my wife Cathy, for always leads first through serving others, and to my daughter Carli, and my son Blake, for always believing in me. You have always inspired me to try to reach to higher levels. I love you! To my mother Charlene Powell, and dad Danny Sr. who at a young age instilled values that I attempt to live in alignment with today. Finally, I would like to acknowledge the work of the co-author of the 2nd edition of this book, and my coaching mentor, Dr. Jon Metz. Without Jon's commitment and dedication, the 2nd edition of Shared Vision would not have been possible.

Danny Powell, 2020

I was humbled and honored when Dr. Powell asked me to be part of this project. I have always admired the culture Danny has built with his team. I hope I can come close to replicating that positive culture and attitude with the teams, athletes, and coaches who I can work with on this incredible journey. When discussing who we wanted to write the foreword for this book, Danny and I both knew Tim Yount was a perfect fit for the task. As Chief Operating Officer at USA Triathlon, Tim, works tirelessly for the sport of triathlon. Especially for the institutions and student-athletes who are part of women's triathlon as an NCAA emerging sport. On a personal level, I would like to thank my parents Douglas and Elizabeth Metz. Living in a family of educators was not always easy, however, with their uncompromising love and support I will be the first member in the history of my family to have a book published. I appreciate the encouragement and resources they provided me while achieving my goals. Finally, I owe Jenny a huge thank you for allowing me to live my dream and believing in me. I will never be able to put into words how much your support means to me.

Jon Metz, 2020

Foreword

By Tim Yount, USA Triathlon

In 2020, I was reminded that it was my 30th year working for USA Triathlon, the governing body for the sport of triathlon and a member of the United States Olympic and Paralympic Committee (USOPC) and the International Triathlon Union (ITU). I recall saying to our staff how gracious I was for the many years of great leadership and a staff that made every day for me something important and relevant to my life.

I was asked about some of the highlights of my time at USA Triathlon. Being a part of the Executive team at the organization since 1992, I had to work through a memorable list of amazing activities and events. There were many but few rivaled my time with our Age Group Team USA athlete, Pan American and Olympic athletes, and the NCAA movement.

My life with Team USA has graced me with the ability to travel the world – over 40 countries and 80 different locations - with athletes representing every state in U.S. I was also chosen to represent the USA as Triathlon Team Leader of our Pan American Games Team in Winnipeg, Canada in 1999 and our Olympic Team in its first Games in Sydney in 2000. In every case, I learned many nuances of leadership and team dynamics all of which shaped the way I led for the organization and the many athletes I was able to represent at the highest level of competition for nearly 20,000 athletes over these three decades. Every team is different so adapting the needs based on the factors of location, size, level of event and time of year certainly played key roles in meeting the level of success desired.

In 2014, one of the most exciting times in USA Triathlon's history took place in San Diego, California. The sport was being voted on the floor of the NCAA Convention by athletic directors representing each divisional level and over 1000 decision makers, as an emerging sport for women. Emerging sports history started in 1994 and was created as a means of helping sport reach NCAA national championship status. The vote of the administrators approved triathlon as an emerging sport by a margin of nearly 94%. After seven years of preparation, this fairly young sport was going to be introduced on an entirely new platform. To say the sport was energized by the newfound position in which we found ourselves, would be a gross understatement.

The program platform build was long and arduous. There were many needs – from the creation of plans for events to scoring of teams, recruitment, and retention. There was also the need for the development of a Coaches Association, a group that would be given the keys to lead the discussions on where the sport should go, led by those programs that were aggressive enough to support the sport in the early years of development. That is when I first engaged with Jon Metz.

Jon Metz had been engrossed in the sport for many years. As a Level II coach, he was already engaged in our programming and was tied do the many things we were doing as a federation with coaching education. His straightforward demeanor and fast charging commitment to the coaching movement was apparent and well timed as we were creating many different layers of a modified coaching program where critical feedback was needed. Jon was engaged and served some important needs for us in that timeframe for the Federation. In 2015, we were fortunate to add Daemen College in NY as our 10th program. Their coach? Jon Metz. This take-charge individual with a doctorate in education, was now not only representing our coaching family in triathlon but one of our first programs under the new NCAA build. It was not long after Jon took over the leadership of the triathlon team at Daemen, that the Varsity Triathlon Coaches Association was created. Its first elected President was Jon Metz. At the time, USA Triathlon had a full time hired staff person working the program. I was engaged as well, supporting the program where gaps existed and working closely with that other administrator and Jon.

Some of the best coaches were born with the gift to lead. That would be Jon. He not only helped craft all of the critically important documents needed for the Coaches Association to be officially legislated but he led a group of coaches through the first stages of true leadership for this young burgeoning sport that was new to the NCAA landscape but not short of motivation to be one of the most impactful emerging sports ever supported at this level. Jon closed out his term limits in 2019 but remains an important part of this continuing build of triathlon as an NCAA emerging sport. He also continues to serve the sport as a specialist to USA Triathlon in the area of coaching education.

About the time that we were building out the Association, another individual named Danny Powell, was named the head coach at Division III Trine, based in Angola, Indiana. With a doctorate in Organizational Management and Associate Professor at Trine University, Danny made an immediate impression on me as someone who was committed to seeing the sport succeed at the NCAA Level. From the onset, Danny built a program that would not only be competitive but a great academic/athletic model for the institution. Athletes engaged in many important builds within the institution. Danny too, with expertise in program design and development, innovative leadership, and organizational behavior, supported the many needs an institution demands with a new program. He built what he as their leader professed was the unified goal.

Danny has been a true gift to the Trine women's varsity triathlon. He has served as a point of inspiration and motivation for the athletes, has represented the program well on the college campus, has earned the respect of his peers in the NCAA triathlon coaching fraternity and has pushed USA Triathlon to be more attentive to needs that represent the entire sport's spectrum. I recall a time when Danny emailed our team and Coaches Association with a concern that was important to not only he and his team but other DIII programs. His push to our staff at USA Triathlon was not misguided - he was compelled to represent for the betterment of the NCAA movement via some changes that were in our collective best interest. It was certainly not singularly motivated. I recall thinking how important this was and thanking him for being so resolute in his passion and drive to assure that it was met head on by USA Triathlon at the point in time even as he was being critical about our actions around the topic. Danny through this one situation, illustrated his command of the sport's commitment to consistent and competent representation and a responsible call for action.

So, as I reflect on the book, Shared Vision, I see the personalities and drive of these two authors through the work they have done in the sport and as coaches and educators on these college campuses. They represent the ideals of vision, values, communication, trust and shared purpose with the teams they have created and impress upon the reader extensions of these key principles that they themselves represent. The book speaks to critical elements we encounter in sport but also see firsthand, in various facets of our lives. Their insights will remind you that we can always learn about ways to improve how we build successful teams, create a level of sustainable success and manage the key decisions that are critical in the pursuit to where we ultimately want to be both personally and professionally.

The NCAA movement wouldn't be where it was without the commitment of many different people – from coaches to volunteers, race directors, athletic institution administrators, the NCAA, athletes and parents. It takes a team approach for a sport to succeed. It requires leadership and common vision at each of these levels to reach the goals the sport has adopted. Shared Vision will remind you of the steps you can take to achieve your desired level of success, and the assurance you need to accomplish what you desire with renewed clarity and intent.

Introduction

"One of the most common and controversial concepts in organizational (and team) psychology is the concept of leadership" (Werth, Markel, & Forster, 2006, p. 102). And though one of the most observed, leadership remains one of the least understood phenomena on earth (Burns, 1978). In fact, as far back as 2500 years ago, the Greek philosopher Socrates wrote volumes on the topic of leadership. To a great extent, Socrates focused on the importance of ethics in his writings. He believed that great leaders honed their craft through lifelong learning, and dialogue not only with other great minds, but also through reflection and self-discovery, always seeking deeper meaning and truth. Plato, a student of Socrates continued the dialogue followed by Aristotle who believed that the ethical role of a leader was not to build their own power, but to create an environment where others could excel, and achieve their full potential. Leaders in our time can learn great lessons through the writings of the "big 3" Greek Philosophers.

Over the centuries, many philosophers, scholars, and others have attempted to understand the subject and dynamics of leadership (Powell, 2010), and as a result the topic of leadership has taken on many meanings and definitions. Some scholars have attempted to find correlations between leadership and performance, while others sought relationships between a leader's behavior and a subordinate's commitment. Still many have spent years attempting to just define this complex topic called leadership. Although **Leadership** has been observed and written about for thousands of years, it remains poorly understood.

Is it any wonder why our history is riddled with tales of leadership atrocities, and stories of immoral ends? We need not look as far back as Machiavelli, Genghis Kahn, Stalin, Hitler, and the like. You just have to look at the global political, corporate, religious, and sport leadership catastrophes of our current time. Many of the historical, and current barbarity, and fiendish corruption resulted from unethical and immoral leadership practices that are incapable of producing extraordinary long-lasting results.

"Great leaders move us, they ignite our passion and inspire the best in us" (Goleman, Boyatzis, & McKee, 2002, p. 3)."Leadership means questioning and challenging the status quo so that outdated unproductive, or socially irresponsible norms can be replaced to meet new challenges" (Daft, 2005, p. 22). In studies conducted by Kouzes and Posner (2007), exemplary leaders, regardless of the type or size of organization they lead, were able to mobilize others to accomplish extraordinary things by engaging in five common practices of effective leadership. Let us take a moment to look at these five common practices.

5 Common Practices of Effective Leadership

1. Model the Way: Having integrity and acting as a role model in both actions and words.
   a. Clarify values by finding your voice and affirming shared ideals.
   b. Set the example by aligning actions and shared values.
2. Inspire a **Shared Vision**: Enthusing others with a vision of how things could be and presenting strategies for attaining this vision.
   a. Envision the future by imagining exciting and ennobling possibilities.
   b. Enlist others in a common vision by appealing to shared aspirations.
3. Challenge the Process: Engaging in ongoing examination of why and how things are done and willingly allowing others to scrutinize and challenge one's own actions.
   a. Search for opportunities by seizing the initiative and looking outward for innovative ways to improve.
   b. Experiment and take risks by constantly generating small wins and learning from experience.

4. Enable Others to Act: Having confidence in the abilities of individuals and enabling them to achieve their potential.
   a. Foster collaboration by building trust and facilitating relationships.
   b. Strengthen others by increasing self-determination and developing competence.
5. Encourage the Heart: Being empathetic to the needs and personalities of individuals and tailoring recognition and feedback to meet these needs and temperament
   a. Recognize contributions by showing appreciation for individual excellence.
   b. Celebrate the values and victories by creating a spirit of community.

These practices characterize **Transformational Leadership** which "occurs when one or more persons engage with others in such a way that leaders and followers raise one another to higher levels of motivation and morality" (Burns, 1978, p. 20). Transformational leaders create meaningful work, promote wellbeing, empower teammates, and increase satisfaction, resulting in increased performance and commitment to the team.

This book, and its related exercises and coursework are written for the use of coaches, administrators, teachers, athletic directors, leadership trainers, and student athletes as a formal leadership development manual. Throughout the book, we will discuss the principles of Transformational Leadership. We will provide reflective assignments for individual team members, team leaders, and coaches to complete and discuss, team exercises that provide opportunities for deliberate practice for many of our leadership principles, and opportunities for team discussion. It has been proven that leadership principles and behaviors can be learned, and it is through the planned and deliberate practice, reflection, and discussion of these principles that individual athletes learn and grow as leaders. It is the sum of individual growth that results in building a culture of leadership within your organization and will ultimately result in a higher level of team cohesion, and performance on and off the field.

Why did we write this book? Most leadership scholars and practitioners agree that exemplary leadership practices and behaviors are practices and behaviors that are learned through experience. Leadership practices and behaviors, which derive long lasting results, are learned through a lifelong deliberate journey of purposeful training, reflection, change, and improvement. We believe that one of the best laboratories to begin this lifelong journey is the court or the field of play. Many life lessons are learned through athletics. Learning how exemplary leaders can change lives and organizations through sport is an effective way of teaching life lessons that will transcend the game and change our world.

We know that in today's increasingly complex and fast changing world, exemplary world changing leadership is in greater demand than ever before. "Effective, long-term world change will not occur through the traditional leadership of power and authority. It will not come through force, coercion, or manipulation. It will come through leadership of an entirely different sort" (Lindsay, 2005, p. 6). It will come through **Transformational Leadership**.

Let's begin!

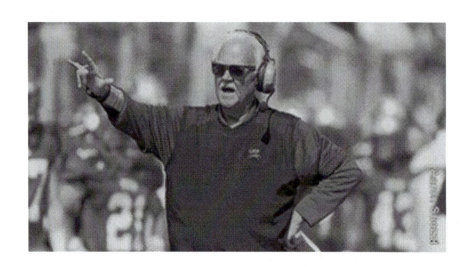

Chapter 1

Leadership

"Leadership is about influence. Nothing more, nothing less."
— John C. Maxwell

Although **Leadership** has been one of the most observed, it remains one of the least understood phenomena on earth. Because the phenomenon of leadership has been so poorly understood, we have lived through most of recorded history with inaccurate myths of what leadership is, and how leaders come to be.

The earliest scientific observations and studies of leadership beginning in the 1960's revolved around what we now refer to as the Trait theories, or Great Man theories. Through the early studies many people have been taught that leaders are born with certain traits and characteristics that are genetic in nature. As you will see over the following pages, we believe leadership is much more than that. There is nothing special about one person's genetic code that makes him or her more superior as a leader than anyone else on a team. We believe we have discovered that leadership is not a place, or a position. There is no secret code for leadership. "Leadership is an observable set of skills and abilities" (Kouzes & Posner, 2008, p. 3).

Observable Leadership Qualities

Leadership as a Trait

The early thought leaders conceptualized leadership to be a trait or set of traits that distinguished the quality of an individual. As a trait, leadership qualities were part of an individual's DNA, and special people were born with or inherited particular traits that made them born leaders. Traits such as confidence, decisiveness, sociability, and intelligence along with many others, are qualities that can influence the way we all lead, but the early opinions were that focusing on traits made leadership a role only for the elite because it implies that only a few people with special talents will lead.

Leadership as an Ability

When viewed as an ability, people are considered able to be a leader, or have the capacity to lead. Though ability can be a natural capacity such as a trait, ability can be acquired as well. For example, some people have the natural physical ability to excel in a particular sport, while others develop their capacity for the sport through practice and exercise. In the same way, many leaders have developed their abilities to lead through hard work and practice.

Leadership as a Skill

When leadership is conceptualized as a skill, it is a competence developed to accomplish a task effectively. Skilled leaders have a competence to understand the means and methods for carrying out their responsibilities. Even more so than ability, conceptualizing leadership as a skill makes leadership available to everyone because skills are aptitudes that people can develop. As a skill, leadership can be studied, practiced, and learned.

Leadership as a Behavior

A behavior is what leaders do when they are in a leadership role. When leadership is conceptualized as behavior, we focus on how leaders behave toward others in various situations in accomplishing objectives. When viewed as behavior, we are able to observe how leaders behave on a continuum of behavior that ranges from task- orientated behavior to relationship-oriented behavior.

For example people natural at task-oriented behaviors may be more naturally inclined to plan, organize, and schedule, while relationship oriented behavior might revolve around helping people feel comfortable in the team, confident in themselves, motivated to accomplish goals, and attend to the emotional side of teammates.

Leadership as a Relationship

When viewed as a relationship, leadership focus is on the communication between leaders and followers rather than just the qualities of the leader. When viewed as a relationship, leadership becomes just as much if not more, about the follower than the leader. In this view of leadership, we believe that the activity of leading is more about focusing on common needs, goals, and objectives in a collaborative process between leaders and followers. As a relationship, leadership is about influence between leader and follower and achieving their collective interests.

Through our research, and the research of many scholars in recent years it has been proven that these observable leadership qualities are a learnable set of practices that given a high level of commitment, **can** be mastered by anyone and everyone on your team.

Leadership is about **learning** and **practicing** these skills and abilities in a way that mobilize others, transform values into actions, and visions into realities. Outstanding team leaders create a climate and culture within a team where obstacles and challenges are renewed into success. Leadership is **everyone's** business! And the opportunities to lead are endless!

Let's begin by defining Leadership. The following are three popular and common definitions of leadership. They may not be yours. What does leadership mean to you?

1. Leadership is the **process** of influencing the activities of others in efforts toward accomplishing a shared vision.
2. Leadership is a relational process of influencing teammates toward individual and common goals, a **shared vision**, and desired end results.
3. Leaders are people who **influence** others by what they say, how they say it and what they do

Exercise 1.1

1. Key Words within These Leadership Definitions: What Do These Words Mean to You?

    a. Process:

    _____
    _____
    _____

    b. Shared Vision:

    _____
    _____
    _____

    c. Relational:

    _____
    _____
    _____

    d. Common Goals:

    _____
    _____
    _____

    e. Influence:

    _____
    _____
    _____

2. Think for a moment about your career as an athlete, or your life in general. Are there any coaches, teachers, relatives, or… that come to mind that you would consider effective leaders?

    _____
    _____
    _____

3. List the characteristics that made these people effective leaders.

_____

_____

_____

4. Now, if you can, identify two or three players that you have known that you would consider effective leaders.

_____

_____

_____

5. List the characteristics that you believe made these players effective leaders.

_____

_____

_____

6. Discuss your experience with leaders who were poor team leaders. Why?

_____

_____

_____

Brief History and Lineage of Leadership Philosophy and Style

A study in 1939 conducted by a research group led by psychologist Kurt Lewin established authoritarian, democratic, and laissez-faire as the three major leadership styles (Lewin, 1939).

Authoritarian

Authoritarian leaders communicate clear expectations for what needs to be accomplished. Additionally, this explicit communication includes when and how it needs to be accomplished. Authoritarian leaders make decisions with little or no input from subordinates while ensuring a distinct separation between themselves and those beneath them on the organizational chart.

Authoritarian leadership can be beneficial when there is not time for shared decision-making. This style is effective when a quick action or decisive decision is needed.

Democratic

Democratic leadership was the most effective among the original three styles identified in the 1939 study. Democratic leaders offer guidance, allow input from others, and remain active participants in the decision-making process. Subordinates under a democratic leader feel engaged, motivated, creative, and provide higher quality contribution because they feel like an integral part of a team working toward common goals.

Laissez-Faire

This delegative style provides limited or no leadership guidance. This form of leadership results in subordinates who lack motivation and do not understand their roles in the organization. However, this leadership style can be beneficial when a group of situational experts are involved.

Additional Leadership Styles

The findings of Lewin's group inspired future research studies that led to the identification of additional leadership styles. Situational, transactional, and transformational are three leadership styles worth noting.

Situational

In 1969 Hersey and Blanchard described a leadership model that was based on the environment and situation. This model provided four distinct leadership styles that include: Telling people what to do; Selling ideas and messages; Participating in the decision-making process; and Delegating most decisions (Hersey, Blanchard, 1969). Future research changed the original model to: Directing with little guidance while expecting obedience; Coaching with plenty of support but giving orders; Supporting with a lot of assistance but little or no direction; and Delegating by providing little or no direction and help (Blanchard, Zigarmi, Zigarmi, 2013).

Transactional Leadership

This style of leadership treats the relationship between the leader and subordinate as a transaction. The biggest benefit of transactional leadership is the clearly defined roles of what needs to be accomplished and what will be the compensation for completing the task. However, this style of leadership will hinder a subordinate's ability to be creative (Hussain S., Et. al. 2017).

Transformational Leadership

This style was identified in the 1970s as leaders who can motivate and inspire subordinates while creating change that is positive. These leaders are emotionally intelligent, committed to achieving organizational goals, and want to help subordinates reach their potential. Research shows that this energetic and passionate style of leadership produces high performing and satisfied subordinates (Choi S.L. Et. al. 2016). Because transformational leadership is considered the most effective leadership style, it will be discussed in greater detail throughout this book.

Individual Exercise 1.2: Leadership Styles Questionnaire

This questionnaire will help to identify your style of leadership and examine how your leadership style relates to other styles of leadership.

1. For each of the statements below, circle the number that indicates the degree to which you agree or disagree (1=strongly disagree and 5=strongly agree). Give your immediate impressions. There are no right or wrong answers.
    a. Employees need to be supervised closely, or they are not likely to do their work.
       1   2   3   4   5
    b. Employees want to be a part of the decision-making process.
       1   2   3   4   5
    c. In complex situations, leaders should let followers work problems out on their own.
       1   2   3   4   5

d. It is fair to say that most employees in the general population are lazy.
    1   2   3   4   5
e. Providing guidance without pressure is the key to being a good leader.
    1   2   3   4   5
f. Leadership requires staying out of the way of followers as they do their work.
    1   2   3   4   5
g. As a rule, employees must be given rewards or punishments in order to motivate them to achieve organizational objectives.
    1   2   3   4   5
h. Most workers prefer supportive communication from their leaders.
    1   2   3   4   5
i. As a rule, leaders should allow followers to appraise their own work.
    1   2   3   4   5
j. Most employees feel insecure about their work and need direction.
    1   2   3   4   5
k. Leaders need to help followers accept responsibility for completing their work.
    1   2   3   4   5
l. Leaders should give followers complete freedom to solve problems on their own.
    1   2   3   4   5
m. The leader is the chief judge of the achievements of the members of the group.
    1   2   3   4   5
n. It is the leader's job to help followers find their passion.
    1   2   3   4   5
o. In most situations, workers prefer little input from the leader.
    1   2   3   4   5
p. Effective leaders give orders and clarify procedures.

1   2   3   4   5

q. People are basically competent and if given a task will do a good job.

1   2   3   4   5

r. In general, it is best to leave followers alone.

1   2   3   4   5

2. Scoring

a. Sum the responses on items 1, 4, 7, 10, 13, and 16 (authoritarian leadership).

b. Sum the responses on items 2, 5, 8, 11, 14, and 17 (democratic leadership).

c. Sum the responses on items 3, 6, 9, 12, 15, and 18 (laissez-faire leadership).

3. Total Scores

a. Authoritarian Leadership _____

b. Democratic Leadership _____

c. Laissez-Faire Leadership _____

4. Scoring Interpretation

This questionnaire is designed to measure three common styles of leadership: authoritarian, democratic, and laissez-faire. By comparing your scores, you can determine which styles are most dominant and least dominant in your own style of leadership.

- If your score is 26–30, you are in the very high range.
- If your score is 21–25, you are in the high range.
- If your score is 16–20, you are in the moderate range.
- If your score is 11–15, you are in the low range.
- If your score is 6–10, you are in the very low range.

Adopted from Northouse, Peter G. Introduction to Leadership: Concepts and practices. Sage. 2015.

Leadership is About Development

Leadership is about development. Leadership is about self-development, as well as developing those around you to achieve their complete potential and become effective leaders. Becoming an effective leader is a lifelong journey that can never be completely mastered. Leadership is a set of learned skills and abilities that must be deliberately practiced to the point of making the practices a habit. Just like shooting a free-throw, repetition enforces habits, and builds muscle memory that can aid in making free-throws a highly predictable shot. A player cannot just read a book to become proficient at shooting free-throws; she must shoot thousands upon thousands of free-throws over a lifetime to become the best shooter she can be. Even then she most likely will still not shoot nearly 100%. This concept holds true in any sport you play, whether it is a tee shot in golf, a serve in tennis, the footwork for an offensive lineman in football, or passing the volleyball. Practice must be deliberate, and reinforce the proper habits and memory, both mentally and physically. Whether you lead a sports organization, or a company, leadership behaviors are learned the same way; deliberate practice, to reinforce proper habits, activities, and behaviors.

Since leadership development is about self-development as well as developing all of those around you, it is critical to create a culture within your team that believes in building a learning organization. Why a learning organization? Because when teams are truly learning, not only are they producing extraordinary results, but the individual members are growing more rapidly than could have occurred independently. Leadership is about creating change, growth, and improvement.

> *"Leadership…lifting a person's vision to higher sights, the raising of a person's performance to a higher standard, the building of a personality beyond its normal limitations."*
> — Peter Drucker

Transformational Leadership

"Effective, long-term world change will not occur through the traditional leadership of power and authority. It will not come through force, coercion, or manipulation. It will come through leadership of an entirely different sort" (Lindsay, 2005, p. 6). The answer: **Transformational Leadership**.

Transformational leadership focuses on actions where both leaders and followers engage in a mutual, ongoing collaborative process of raising one another to higher levels of motivation, cohesion, and performance. Leaders behave in ways that motivate their teammates by appealing to the values, beliefs, and attitudes of followers.

Transformational team leaders are concerned with a team's forward movement, setting a direction, sharing a vision, transforming values into action, turning obstacles into innovations, risks into rewards, and uniting individuals in a common purpose. This type of approach builds respect and trust throughout the organization, resulting in fearless followership and team commitment. Transformational leaders direct and sustain change for the greater good of the team and has proven to result in higher performance.

> *"In your preparation to take on the task of helping others enlarge themselves, the first thing you need to do is to improve and enlarge yourself because only when you are growing and enlarging yourself are you able to help others do the same."*
> — *John C. Maxwell*

Individual Exercise 1.3: Your Best Leadership Experience

With leadership, as with many things in life, experience is the best teacher. Most leaders learn what to do by trying it themselves or by watching others. The problem is that not all of what is done or observed is appropriate. So, it's important for you to base your leadership practices on the best of what you do or see-those times when you've done your best as a leader or when you've observed others at their personal best. Such examples provide role models for effective leadership.

1. Recall a time when, in your opinion, you did your very best as a leader of other people. Your leadership experience can be with your present team or a previous one. It can be as an appointed, selected, or emerged leader. Write a very brief description of that experience below.

   _____

   _____

   _____

   _____

2. Think about the choice you just made and use the space provided to summarize five to seven things you did as a leader. Consider how you led, what actions you took, and what caused this leadership experience to be your personal best.

    a. _____

    b. _____

    c. _____

    d. _____

    e. _____

    f. _____

    g. _____

3. What words describe the character (the quality, nature, personality, tone, special mood, etc.) of this experience?

    _____
    _____
    _____
    _____

4. Now interview three people who know you well (teammates, family, friends), and ask them if they have witnessed you in a position of leadership, or an activity where you have displayed leadership. Have them explain why they believe that this is in their opinion, your personal best leadership experience.

    a. What actions did they see you take?

        _____
        _____
        _____
        _____

b. What words describe the character of this experience?

_____

_____

_____

_____

5. What would you say were the major lessons about leadership that you learned from this experience? What common actions, qualities, and character traits do you see in your own personal best leadership experience, and what others witnessed as your personal best leadership experiences?

_____

_____

_____

_____

6. Finally, have you witnessed someone in your life that displays exemplary leadership qualities (family, coach, teacher, teammate, friend, other)? Describe the qualities that you see in them, that create a sense of **fearless followership** in your mind? In other words, why would you follow them in the most difficult of times?

_____

_____

_____

_____

This exercise is an adaptation of Kouzes, J M., Posner, B Z. (2003). Leadership Challenge: Personal-Best Leadership Questionnaire [Short Form].

You Cannot Improve without Change

You will be confronted with change in every dimension of your life. Change affects nearly every aspect of even the natural world around us. Sunrise follows sunset, fall follows summer, which follows spring. There is the natural progression of life, evident in birth and death, abundance and need, success and failure. Though many people focus on the negative aspects of change due to its difficult nature, change is instrumental in bringing about growth and improvement (Smith, 2001).

You cannot improve without change. To become better or improve at doing something, you must be deliberate in making some kind of change in the way you have previously done the activity. We have all heard that the definition of insanity is doing the same thing over and over again but expecting different results. Well, improving as a professional or an athlete is the same way. Whether you want to become a better leader, pitcher, offensive lineman, student, teammate, coach, or stockbroker, you must deliberately make changes in some aspect of your life to make the improvements that you want to see.

Changes that can result in desired improvements and lasting results may involve many areas of your life such as your knowledge, the people you hang out with, your habits, your mindset, your physical skills, or the effort and dedication you put into training, practice, and personal growth.

In order to be successful at making desired improvements it is critical to understand to what extent each specific change correlates to better performance, and improvement. In other words, you must ask yourself these questions:

1. What kind of improvements do I want to make?
2. What performance measurements will I use to measure those improvements?
3. What changes are necessary to make these improvements?

Setting Goals

Setting goals for improvement and growth are important, but it is equally important to have a process to monitor and measure those goals for desired results so that you can have evidence of the impact of your hard work. It is in this area that most athletes fail.

Holding Yourself Accountable

Holding yourself accountable is critical and is the key to successful change. For example, personal goals to improve your speed and agility are all well and good, but if the goals are ignored, and a deliberate process put into place, change will not occur. It does not matter how many lofty goals you set as an athlete or a professional if you have no way of measuring or assessing your effectiveness.

Plan Change in Specific Terms

It is important to plan change in specific terms. Do not think in general terms like, "I want to become a better leader". Be much more specific than that. For example, think "Every time I catch a teammate thinking negatively, I will help him find the positives in the situation." Or "When I see a teammate get down on herself after a bad play, I will pick her up and encourage her to learn from that play to become a better player". Or "I will deliberately recognize the contributions of my teammates by showing appreciation for individual excellence".

Change and Improvement Goals Must be Realistic

Change and improvement goals must be realistic. Successful, long lasting changes are usually built upon small, measurable, well planned incremental steps rather than one large all-or-nothing goal. It is the deliberate practice of accomplishing small well-planned goals, which accumulate to result in big changes.

The Five Dimensions of Change

In order to create lasting change successfully, five factors must be addressed. Making meaningful change in our lives successful requires us to have a calling to change, the desire to change, the knowledge necessary to make the change, must make the effort to change, and must be in an environment that encourages the change.

Spiritual: Your Calling to Change

The spiritual dimension relates to your value system, and your grounded center. This factor is focused on the unshakable sources that inspire and uplift you. This is your inspiration, or inner calling that is urging you to be at your best. Changing your spiritual self through meditation, prayer, service, spending time in nature, and reflection has been proven to facilitate and increase your capacity to handle challenges around you.

Emotional: Your Desire to Change

The emotional dimension relates to your impassioned desire to change. This impassioned desire is fed by your spiritual calling, and dissatisfaction with the way things are in their current state. At this stage, you have identified that you need to improve, and grow into a more effective team leader and team player.

Mental: The Knowledge Necessary to Implement the Change

The mental dimension relates to understanding not only what you want to change, but also understanding the specific steps necessary to make your change successful. Many efforts to change fail simply because student athletes, professionals, and organizations lack the knowledge needed to successfully implement the change. It is important to expose yourself to great minds, and keep your own mind sharp through reading, planning, and organizing. You are currently taking a meaningful step in broadening your knowledge to initiate positive change by taking this course.

Physical: Your Readiness, Willingness, and Effort to Change

The physical dimension relates to how you have prepared your physical being to endure the stress and pressure that will help you improve through personal change and improvement. There are no shortcuts to becoming the best athlete, or the best leader you can be. Becoming the best athlete, and the best leader you can be requires intense effort and is an ongoing process. Having the desire to change and the knowledge to implement the change is not enough. Improvement will not happen unless you are ready and willing to apply great effort. The physical dimension involves paying attention to your physical body by exercising properly, eating properly, getting enough rest, and preparing for optimal performance.

Social: Your Relationships with Others

The social dimension relates to the relationships and environment around you. Having healthy relationships with your teammates and peers is critical to creating an environment that supports and encourages change. Though you cannot control every element within your environment, you can work toward building a culture where unity, growth, excellence, and values driven goals are encouraged and supported. Unity stresses community and teamwork, with words such as "we" and "us". It is very important that you carefully build your change environment as best as possible.

Team Exercise 1.1

Team Leader – With your teammates:

1. On the following pages list of all the things which are factors that promote change and improvement for individual team members and for the team in each of the five dimensions of change.
2. Make a list of factors that hinder change and improvement for individual team members and for the team in each of the five dimensions of change.
3. Discuss the factors that promote change and improvement in each of the five dimensions of change. Ask questions like: Why do they exist? How do they make our team better?
4. In the spirit of the saying, "As good as we are, how will we get better?" what 3-5 actions are we willing to take to remove the things that hinder change and improvement?
5. Pick a team spokesperson to discuss your thoughts and findings.

Individual Factors That Promote Change

- Spiritual

  _____

  _____

- Emotional

  _____

  _____

- Mental

  _____

  _____

- Physical

  _____

  _____

- Social

  _____

  _____

Team Factors That Promote Change

- Spiritual

  _____

  _____

- Emotional

  _____

  _____

- Mental

  _____

  _____

- Physical

  _____

  _____

- Social

  _____

  _____

Individual Factors that Hinder Change

- Spiritual

  _____

  _____

- Emotional

  _____

  _____

- Mental

_____

_____

- Physical

_____

_____

- Social

_____

_____

Team Factors that Hinder Change

- Spiritual

_____

_____

- Emotional

_____

_____

- Mental

_____

_____

- Physical

_____

_____

- Social

_____

_____

This exercise is an adaptation of Dobbs, C. (2009). SCRIMMAGE! Team Exercise, "You Cannot Improve without Change: Making Successful Changes in Your Life". Premier Graphics Publishing.

Chapter 1 Notes

Chapter 2

Inspiring a Shared Purpose

"Where there is no vision, the people perish."
— *Proverbs 29:18 KJV*

Ideal Future

On November 19th in 1863, about 4 months after the Union defeated the Union forces in the battle of Gettysburg, Abraham Lincoln presented what we now call the Gettysburg Address, and became one of the best known speeches in American history. Though this wasn't the primary speech of that day, in just about 270 words, President Lincoln painted a picture of an ideal future that others believed to be possible. This speech painted a picture of an ideal future state that others believed to be better than their present state, motivating masses of United States Citizens to mobilize toward a common goal of unity, freedom, and revolved around the Declaration of Independence (Lincoln, 1863). Though President Lincoln only spoke for a few short minutes, he described an ideal future that others wanted to be a part of, and greatly united a divided country.

During President Kennedy's Inaugural Address (Kennedy, 1961), JFK discussed an ideal future for his constituents, greatly uniting his country in moving toward a future state that was stronger and better than the then current state when he said "undo the heavy burdens…and let the oppressed go free". This speech became, and remains, popular because of the President's "ask not what your country can do for you--ask what you can do for your country" statement, mobilizing millions of Americans to work toward moving to a future that is bright and inclusive.

In September of 1962, JFK declared that within the next decade, "we choose to go to the moon" (Kennedy, 1962). Something we currently thought impossible, it was declared during the cold war, we would accomplish. Though we were confident we could send men into space, we had no idea how to land on the moon, and even more, had no idea how to get them back to earth. To put things into context, it was believed during the time that controlling space and the moon would allow those first people to control the cold war. JFK excited the USA to envision a future that was better than its current state.

On August 28th of 1963, framed by the Gettysburg Address, and anchored by the Lincoln Monument, Dr. Martin Luther King Jr. presented what we now call the "I Have a Dream" speech. Dr. King spoke for just around 17 minutes, and again used this time to present an idea of a future state that mobilized millions of Americans to transform the way we viewed equality. Just as President Lincoln, Dr. King painted a picture of a future that was better than where we were currently as a civilization. It was an ideal future that mobilized masses. In Dr. King's words "I have a Dream", he articulated a **vision**, of an ideal future, that others were able to see themselves being a part of. An ideal future that allowed them to see themselves being a part of. A futures state that was better than the current state (King, 1963).

One of the most distinguishing characteristics of an exemplary Transformational Leader lies in their ability to paint a compelling picture of an organization's ideal future. When they paint the picture, they communicate it in a way that allows their teammates to see themselves playing an integral role in the organization's success, and achievement of organizational goals.

The ideal future of an organization is defined by a vision of the ultimate destination and purpose for the organization. This destination and organizational purpose, acts as a compass for your organization, showing the direction toward your ideal future. Exemplary Transformational Leaders have learned how to share this vision of the future with teammates in a way that mobilizes a guiding coalition by building a synergy of collective energy and commitment whereby each team member is inspired and energized to strive for the collective aspirations of the team (Smith, 2001).

The examples above allowed the authors to speak to the hearts and minds of their constituents. They spoke to the collective aspirations of our society.

As a result, enabled masses of individuals to see a future that they wanted to be a part of, and mobilized them to struggle to achieve it.

As the guiding compass of the organization as the aforementioned examples demonstrate, your vision should be value driven, principle centered, and focused on the purpose of the organization. A clear vision of your organization's ideal future should convict, inspire, and enable individuals and their teams to attain peak performance and achieve extraordinary goals (Covey, 1991, Kouzes, 2008, Smith, 2001). These principles are not only meaningful in politics and in the greater society, but as you will see during the work that you will do throughout this book, in the locker room and the boardroom.

Shared Vision

When a leader successfully builds a coalition of teammates that are mobilized, energized, inspired, and committed to a common purpose, that leader has accomplished the goal of creating a **shared vision** for her/his organization. A **shared vision** gets everyone in the organization on the same page and committed to the success of a common goal.

When Marquette went to the Final Four in 2003 while Dwayne Wade was a teammate, a national sportswriter asked Bill Cords, athletic director, about whether their appearance was an anomaly, or an aberration. Mr. Cords stated "It's neither one. It is a great example of what people can do if they are all on the same page, have the same expectations, and are all committed to success" (Crean, 2007). Inspiring a **shared vision** requires envisioning the future, by imagining exciting and ennobling possibilities, and enlisting others in a common purpose by appealing to shared aspirations (Kouzes & Posner, 2007).

Vision is Critical

Bennis and Nanus have said vision is a mental image of a possible and desirable future state. Vision sets direction and promotes action by crystallizing creative thought and defining our future. By reaching for the impossible, vision allows dreams to become reality, and when effectively conceptualized and communicated, vision brings order to chaos (Smith, 2001).

> *"For me, winning isn't something that happens suddenly on the field when the whistle blows and the crowds roar. Winning is something that builds physically and mentally every day that you train and every night that you dream."*
> — *Emmitt Smith*

The primary reason vision is critical is because without a clear vision of our **ideal future** we tend to be reactionary, taking a seat-of-the-pants approach to handling one crisis after another, and becoming dependent on directions from others. While a clearly defined vision based on a guiding purpose, empowers, and enables teammates to seize the initiative and look for innovative ways to improve, increasing self-determination, and developing competence. Clearly defined, well communicated, internalized visions mobilize, and energize teammates to grow and improve as individuals, and ultimately promote collaboration, and the collective purpose of your team.

Envision the Future

> *"To succeed...You need to find something to hold on to, something to motivate you, something to inspire you."*
> — *Tony Dorsett*

Organizations are in critical need of visionary leaders. Creating a vision for your organization takes imagination, and the courage to reach for the stars and visualize what your organization will be like when it is accomplishing its highest-level goals.

Visionary leaders ask: "what is the absolute best I can imagine for our organization?" (Smith, 2001, p. 99).

Proactive leaders need to set the stage for what is to come, and be curious by asking: "what if?", "how can we?", and "what if we?" Stephen Covey believes that effective leaders begin with the end in mind (Covey, 1991). Beginning a football season or a volleyball season with the end results in mind (like winning the conference championship, or a national title) sounds like an elementary idea, but it is shocking how few leaders and teams have crystalized the picture of their ideal future in a way that each step toward their desired end is purposeful, values driven, principle centered, and internalized throughout the organization.

The following exercise is a visualization activity. The purpose of this activity is to allow you as a leader and team mate to vividly paint a picture of the future state you desire. Do not be afraid to "dream" during this activity. This is your ideal future!

As you are visualizing during this exercise, try to use all your senses. By using all your senses, you are more accurately and clearly able to imagine your future goals. By exercising all of your senses, think about what you smell, what sounds you hear, what emotions you are feeling, what your body feels like. Be vivid and be specific. Can you smell the popcorn in the gymnasium? Can you hear your fans cheer? Can you smell the freshly cut grass? Do you feel the sweat running down your face? As you begin to answer each question, close your eyes, and actually see it.

Exercise 2.1

Let's begin envisioning your future for this team.

1. What 10 things do you want to accomplish this season as an athlete? As a team?

   a. _____

   b. _____

   c. _____

   d. _____

   e. _____

   f. _____

   g. _____

   h. _____

i. _____

j. _____

2. What 10 things do you want to accomplish during your career on this team?

    a. _____

    b. _____

    c. _____

    d. _____

    e. _____

    f. _____

    g. _____

    h. _____

    i. _____

    j. _____

3. In 5 years, when you look back on what you have done, what will you say about this journey?

_____
_____
_____
_____

    a. Where will you be?

_____
_____
_____

b. What are you doing?

_____

_____

_____

4. What will others say about this journey?

_____

_____

_____

_____

5. What do you want your current teammates to remember about this journey, what will they say?

_____

_____

_____

_____

6. What do you want your team's legacy to be?

_____

_____

_____

_____

7. What do you want your legacy to be as a player, a teammate, a leader, a follower?

_____

_____

_____

_____

8. What differences will there be in the ways current and future teams work and live because of your influence and your contribution to this team?

_____

_____

_____

_____

Chapter 2 Notes

Chapter 3

Values Matter

Values are the things that you believe are important in the way you live, play, and work. They (should) determine your priorities, and, deep down, they're probably the way you tell yourself you are living in alignment with the way you want to. How do you know this? When the things that you do and the way you behave match your values, life is usually good – you're satisfied and content. But when these don't align with your personal values, that's when things feel... wrong. This can be a real source of unhappiness, and results in what we refer to as cognitive dissonance. Cognitive dissonance is defined as a phenomenon when behaviors and beliefs do not align.

People create and develop their own set of values throughout the course of their lives. Experiences and interactions with family, peers, culture, and society contribute to the values that an individual holds. Values are a person's principles or standards of behavior. Values influence how we live our life, conduct ourselves, our judgement, and our decision-making process. Some additional sources that values can be derived from include: the workplace; educational institutions, significant life events, religion, music, and media.

Values are the non-debatable, and non-compromise-able truths that direct our behavior. Values are the motivational force that direct our reasons for doing things, and at the same time set boundaries around our behavior, restricting us from doing other things. Larry Lindsay believed that core values are the filter through which vision development must pass and core values are what govern daily life (Smith, 2001).

It is important that leaders understand what they value. These values will be important in informing your relationships with superiors, colleagues, and subordinates. When we are aware of our core values, we have a benchmark to:

- ask why we are doing what we are doing
- identify the consequences of our actions
- consider alternative options

In addition to understanding your values, as a leader, it is important to know your values impact your beliefs and your beliefs impact your behavior.

"Ask not what your teammates can do for you. Ask what you can do for your teammates."
— Magic Johnson

Values are so important to leadership that when King David talked about values in Psalm 15 (New International Version). He said that leaders who value truth, kindness, honesty, and justice will never be shaken. David mentions four core values, but there are probably many more that act as your guiding compass. Though King David mentioned truth, kindness, honesty, and justice, the list of things we consider values is long. Here are a few examples of recent leaders:

> Legendary UCLA basketball coach John Wooden discussed his personal values as being his lifelong guides. Coach Wooden said that he was taught the importance of values from his Father growing up and practiced them throughout life. His core values were family, faith, and friends (Wooden, 1997).

> Mike Krzyzewski (Coach K) of Duke University identifies the core values of Duke Basketball as trust, collective responsibility, caring, communication, and pride. During Marquette's run to the Final Four under Coach Crean, their core values were identified as "integrity, respect, responsibility, unselfishness, loyalty, and tenacity" (Crean, 2007, p. 59).

Dean Smith believed that his North Carolina Tarheels basketball team was "built on the tenets of integrity, honor, respect, and loyalty" (Crean, 2007, p. 19).

West Point Cadets' shared values are duty, honor, and country.

What sets these organizations apart from their many other competitors, and what has made these teams into consistent high performing organizations, is that these stated values are not just words. These values are actually communicated and passionately internalized, believed in, and passionately lived out by every teammate, every day.

These values are written. These values are published. These values are spoken with pride. These values are posted in the locker rooms, the hallways, and offices for everyone to see, read, and memorize. They have become a critical part of the internal fabric of each team, and each team member is accountable to abide in them.

All authentic leaders identify, understand, and to their best ability allow themselves to be guided by their values. It is not by accident that these leaders consistently produce teams that out-perform their competition.

What drives these leaders is something much larger than self. These leaders understand the importance that **shared values** play in building a cohesive team that will endure the inevitable tough season, will overcome adversity, and will pull together during difficult times, because they are guided by a selfless desire to the team driven vision. Where do these values come from? How did these individuals realize these values? Why do these values become important in the way they lead?

The next exercise allows you to explore influences in your life. Why is this important? Who were major influencers? Why?

Individual Exercise 3.1

1. Below are a few areas in which you may hold values. Score each area on a 1-10 scale (1=no value at all and 10=extremely high value). What are some of the values you hold in these areas?
   a. Manners – Do manners have value in your life?
      1 2 3 4 5 6 7 8 9 10
   b. Pride – Are there things you need to be proud of?
      1 2 3 4 5 6 7 8 9 10
   c. Clothes – Is what you wear important?
      1 2 3 4 5 6 7 8 9 10
   d. Family – Do you value family?
      1 2 3 4 5 6 7 8 9 10

2. Athletic Behavior – What athletic behaviors do you value? (e.g. sportsmanship, fair play, winning, team culture, individual performance, etc.) Why?

   _____

   _____

   _____

   _____

Team Exercise 3.1

Discuss with your teammates the same questions found in Individual Exercise 3.1. Do the answers differ?

_____

_____

_____

_____

Individual Exercise 3.2: Identifying My Personal Values

In the previous chapter you were asked to visualize your **ideal future**, personal and team accomplishments, and the legacy you and your team will leave behind. Now we want you to revisit those questions, reflect deeply on your answers, and complete the following:

1. Based on this reflection, list 15-20 ideals, or core values that you consider important to your personal character, and that of the team. What things do you want people to recognize about you, and remember about you, and could be a great characteristic of the nature and culture of this team? (Honorable, Trustworthy, Friend, Confidant, Expert, Humble, Servant, Undeniable Will, Humility, Integrity, Teamwork, Responsibility, Being Productive, Communication, Cooperation. See appendix 1 for more examples). Don't be afraid to dream. Ask yourself; what are the most important principles in life? What grounds me? What will I not compromise?

   _____

   _____

   _____

   _____

   _____

   _____

   _____

   _____

   _____

2. Reflect on this list of 15-20 core ideals. Rank the top 5 that are unshakeable, non-debatable, and non-compromise-able, reflecting the person that you would most want to be.

   _____

   _____

   _____

   _____

3. Think of the one, two, or three people that you admire most in this world, how would they feel about this list? What values do you see in them? Why?

   _____

   _____

   _____

   _____

4. As a result of this list, will those around me become better? If so, in what ways?

_____

_____

_____

_____

_____

5. Reflect once again on the vision for yourself, and your team in the previous section. Based on identifying the core values that drive your actions. Write a statement in fewer than 200 words that reflects your vision for this team.

_____

_____

_____

_____

_____

6. Finally, reflecting on your previous statement. You will begin to draft your personal Mission Statement. As succinctly as possible (less than 50 words) write a statement that addresses how the 3-5 most unshakeable, non-debatable, and non-compromise-able values will be lived out in your life. This draft might be a work in progress but should eventually be perfected to a statement that is memorized, internalized, and lived out.

_____

_____

_____

_____

_____

Chapter 3 Notes

Chapter 4

Is the Vision Shared by Your Teammates?

"Leadership is not simply about what you want for yourself; it is also about what others want for themselves. Exemplary leaders understand the hopes and dreams of their constituents, and they are able to forge a unity of common aspirations. It's this collective understanding of a mutually desirable future that inspires people to share a common vision of the future" (Kouzes & Posner, 2008, p. 51).

Leaders

In many cases, leaders assume that it is **their vision** that best drives an organization forward and that since it is their vision, they must be the one who creates it. Though leaders are expected to begin with the end in mind, and envision the possibilities for the future, it is necessary that leaders understand that they cannot effectively **impose their vision** of the future on others.

> *"The way a team plays, as a whole, determines its success. You may have the greatest bunch of individual stars in the world, but if they don't play together, the club won't be worth a dime."*
> — *Babe Ruth*

Teammates

Teammates have aspirations and dreams to be fulfilled. Teammates want to participate in a vision where they can really visualize those dreams and aspirations coming true. Your teammates want to see a picture of the future in a way that they see themselves as part of the future, and their role as being an important contributor in one way or another. The very best leaders know that imposing their own vision on others. The very best leaders know that their job is to inspire a **shared vision** for the future.

"I've worked too hard and too long to let anything stand in the way of my goals. I will not let my teammates down, and I will not let myself down"
— Mia Hamm

You cannot motivate people to willingly take a journey they don't want to take. When visions are shared, they withstand the challenges of a long season's journey, they are better able to maintain high levels of motivation through the season and long off-season, and they create a higher level of cohesion, attracting more people to the cause.

Building a Vision

"Sports creates a bond between contemporaries that lasts a lifetime. It also gives your life structure, discipline and a genuine, sincere, pure fulfillment that few other areas of endeavor provide."
— Bob Cousy

Let's begin to drill into building a vision that is shared with your coaches and teammates, by exploring the dreams, ambitions, and values of your coaches and teammates. To do this, it will be necessary to set an appointment to interview your coach. During this appointment, you will get to know the coach better, and you will explore her/his expectations for you as a team leader, a follower, and a teammate. You will also spend time talking about his/her hopes, dreams, and the top five values she/he advocates for your team. In addition, you should get to know your teammates better. Spend time with a minimum of 10 teammates, and engage in a conversation about their dreams, aspirations, and core unshakeable values. To help you through the interview process, use the following questionnaires to build a portfolio (Dobbs, 2009).

Individual Exercise 4.1: Coach's Profile

Getting to know your coaches can be critically important and can help you become an exemplary team leader. Understanding who your coach is, her/his background, goals, and unshakable core values, will help you to understand your role as a leader and follower on this team, as well as help you to crystalize and communicate a **shared vision**, and a **shared purpose** for this team.

1. Coach Profile:
   a. Coach

   _____

   b. Position

   _____

   c. Coaching Background (years coaching, sports coaches etc.)

   _____

   d. Core Values

   _____

   e. Favorite Leaders/Why?

   _____

2. Coach Values Questionnaire:
   a. What are the 5 critical values you champion for our team?

   _____
   _____
   _____
   _____
   _____

   b. What are your expectations of team leaders?

   _____
   _____
   _____

   c. What are your expectations for me as a team leader?

_____
_____
_____

    d. What are the critical few standards for which you will daily hold me accountable? (What's Important NOW?)

_____
_____
_____

    e. How will I be held accountable for these standards?

_____
_____
_____

3. Team Goals:

    a. What goals do you have for our team?

_____
_____
_____

    b. What role do you see me playing in our team goals?

_____
_____
_____

    c. How can I communicate our goals to my teammates?

_____
_____
_____

Individual Exercise 4.2: Team Member Profile

Creating a cohesive unit and creating a shared purpose for your team requires getting to know your teammates. You are going to make a journey together. During this journey, you will celebrate victories together, and you will also rely on each other to pull through the tough times. In order to become an exemplary team leader, you must be prepared by having awareness and understanding of who your teammates are. This understanding will help you crystalize, communicate, and keep one another focused on the **shared vision**, and the **shared purpose** for this team.

1. Teammate Profile:
    a. Teammate

    _____

    b. Position

    _____

    c. Year: Freshman, Sophomore, Junior, Senior (circle one)

    d. Athletic Background

    _____

    e. Core Values

    _____
    _____
    _____

    f. What are the 2-3 things that really inspire and motivate this teammate? Why?

    _____
    _____
    _____

    g. Short and Long-Term Goals

    _____
    _____
    _____

Chapter 4 Notes

Chapter 5

Communication, Communication, Communication

"You don't lead by pointing and telling people some place to go. You lead by going to that place and making a case."
— Ken Kesey

Communication is essential to extraordinary transformational leadership. To become an effective leader, it will become necessary to learn how to share ideas and transmit a sense of urgency and enthusiasm in a way that the complicated becomes simple. Communication is the tool that enables you as a leader to enlist others in a common purpose.

Without the ability to communicate in a way that enlists, inspires, and creates urgency in others, you will travel alone. Though there are teams full of individuals traveling alone, extraordinary teams know that communicating effectively turns a divided focus into a **shared vision**. Extraordinary leaders know that communicating effectively means appealing to others' hopes and dreams and painting the picture in a way that their teammates see how their dreams will come true.

"Effective teamwork begins and ends with communication."
— Mike Krzyzewski

A great deal of literature states that the most important qualities in a leader directly relate to the virtues of trust, and integrity. However, the most distinguishing characteristic of great leaders, and the hardest quality to find in an executive is the ability to communicate. Not just talk at people, but engage in the type of communication that unites, inspires, and recruits teammates to join forces and achieve extraordinary things.

It must be noted that the ability to communicate does not discount the virtues of trust, and integrity. To the contrary in fact, it amplifies the importance of trust, and integrity. How can you believe the message if you don't believe the messenger?

Communication is not easy. Communication does not always come naturally. Like many other functions of leadership, communication must be learned, and deliberately practiced to become proficient. Many, many top executives have become aware of this over the years, and as a result they commit to a lifelong journey of deliberately putting themselves in situations that require them to practice their communication skills.

In order to effectively communicate with your teammates, it is critical that you know how to talk to one another, as well as know how to listen to one another. Oddly, listening is most often the most important part of the equation. We've been told God gave us two ears, and one mouth for a reason.

Have you ever told somebody something and by the time it gets back to you, the story is completely changed? Here is an example.

A College President told the Chief Information Officer the following:

> *"Next Thursday at 10:30 a.m., Halley's Comet will appear over this area. This is an event which occurs only once every 75 years. Call the Athletic Director and have him assemble the coaches and athletes on the athletic field and explain this phenomenon to them. If it rains, cancel the day's activities and have the athletes meet in the gymnasium to see a film about the comet."*

The Chief Information Officer naturally said yes. He was to pass that exact same message, word-for-word, on to the athletic director, but this is what the Chief Information Officer heard:

> *"By order of the President, next Thursday at 10:30 a.m., Halley's Comet will appear on your athletic field. If it rains, cancel the day's activities and report to the gymnasium with your coaches and athletes*

where you will be shown films, a phenomenal event which occurs only once every 75 years."

The Athletic Director was asked to pass this on to the Coaches. This is what the Coaches heard:

"By order of the phenomenal College President, at 10:30 a.m., next Thursday, Halley's Comet will appear in the gymnasium. In case of rain on the athletic field, the President will give another order, something which occurs only once every 75 years."

The Coaches were asked to pass this message on to the Athletes. This is what the Athletes heard:

"Next Thursday at 10:30 a.m., the College President will appear in our gymnasium with Halley's Comet, something which occurs only once every 75 years. If it rains, the President will cancel the comet and have us all meet on our phenomenal athletic field."

Finally, the Athletes were asked to take this information to their Parents. This is what the Parents heard from the Athletes:

"When it rains next Thursday at 10:30 a.m., over the athletic field, the phenomenal 75-year-old College President will cancel all activities and will appear before the whole college in the gymnasium accompanied by Bill Hailey and the Comets."

"I always tell kids, you have two eyes and one mouth. Keep two open and one closed. You never learn anything if you're the one talking."
— *Gordie Howe*

Know Your Teammates

In order to understand how to talk to your teammates, and how to listen to your teammates, it is essential to know your teammates. "Leadership is not a solo act, it's a team effort" (Kouzes & Posner, 2007, p. 223). Leadership involves the support of many people. To engage that support, it is essential to remember that leadership is a **relationship**. All successful long-term relationships involve gaining a knowledge about, and understanding of, the others involved in the relationship. It is very difficult to effectively communicate with someone, or a group of people you do not know, or who do not know you. Without knowledge, there is little relationship. Without a relationship, why would anyone care about the success of their teammates?

Accomplishing Team Goals

To accomplish team goals, teammates must rely on each other, cooperate, collaborate, and build a climate of interdependence. This climate of interdependence involves creating a culture that understands that they cannot succeed unless everyone succeeds.

John Maxwell called the art of knowing and understanding people, having a "leader's head". Maxwell believed that people have several things in common: (Maxwell, 1999, p. 107).

- They like to feel special, so sincerely compliment them.
- They want a better tomorrow, so show them hope.
- They desire direction, so navigate for them.
- They are selfish, so speak to their needs first.
- They get low emotionally, so encourage them.
- They want success, so help them win.

Knowing your teammates and understanding their needs, wants, and desires, will allow you to communicate with them in a way that addresses these higher-level needs.

The exercises that you completed in the last chapter allowed you to have an opportunity to talk with members of your team as well as members of your coaching staff. Those exercises were meant to accomplish two things. The first thing that it was meant to accomplish, was to guide us closer to defining common values, goals, dreams, and visions for our future. The second thing that the exercises were meant to accomplish was to help you know and understand each other better. Not just from a superficial standpoint, but from the standpoint of understanding our higher-level desires and needs; the real things that motivate us. Truly understanding these needs, desires, and motivational drivers requires really listening. Listening with the desire to truly understand.

The next exercise will help you sharpen your listening skills with the desire to truly understand.

Individual Exercise 5.1: Listen to Your Teammates

1. Think of a time when someone **really** listened to you.
   a. What did that person do?

   _____

   _____

   b. What did he or she say?

   _____

   _____

   c. What was the effect on you? How did it make you feel?

   _____

   _____

2. I am interested in my teammate's plans.
   Not at All..Very
       1   2   3   4   5

3. I listen to my teammates when they are talking.
   Never   Always
       1   2   3   4   5

4. I try to understand the perspective of my teammates.
   Never   Always
       1   2   3   4   5

5. What do you do to give people opportunities to be heard?

   _____

   _____

   _____

Simplify Your Message

Being able to effectively communicate is one of the most important skills we can learn in life. We spend most of our life trying to do it in one way or another; writing, speaking, reading, listening, watching, doing... Yet it is shocking how few resources we dedicate to the **deliberate** training and practicing of these vital skills. We must come to a place where we understand the importance of communication, and its role in truly understanding our peers; and the role communication plays in bringing our teammates together to achieve a common goal.

Consequently, the essential brand of communication necessary to turn a group of individuals with different backgrounds, talents, and ideas into a cohesive team that can effectively talk and listen, both on and off the field of play is very rare.

Many times, simplifying your message becomes the critical task for effective communication. Great communicators are excellent at making their message easy to understand. Effective communicators break a message down in a way that leaves little to interpretation and misinterpretation. They are very clear in their message.

The most effective communication is many times made clear through more than just the spoken word. Effective communication happens as a result of partnering the spoken word with **symbols**, **artifacts**, and **pictures** that stir emotion, and resonate with the organization. We have all heard the saying, "a picture paints a thousand words". Well, simplifying a message by turning words into pictures, symbols, and artifacts enables a leader to turn complex messages, or concepts into a simple mental picture.

Effective communication creates a sense of urgency to the common goals and shared aspirations, by addressing your teammate's higher-level needs. Effective communication results in ownership of the common vision, goals, and mission of your organization and turns a group of individuals into a true **team**. This is best accomplished when the message is crystal clear.

In 2003, Dr. Powell had an opportunity to listen to a presentation given by Coach Krzyzewski at College of the Ozarks. Coach K talked about leadership that night, but the most critical piece of his 90-minute presentation was how he used "the fist" as a symbol to communicate a critical message that is the essence of Duke's values, and organizational mission. This was a complex message, simplified down to one symbol that everyone understood very clearly.

Each separate finger that makes "the fist", not only symbolizes one of the five players on the floor at any given time, but also symbolizes each of the five core values that Duke basketball is built upon; communication, trust, collective responsibility, care, and pride. The symbol of "the fist" expresses without words that five fingers held together in a tight fist is far more effective and powerful than five fingers held outstretched alone. Not only are five players working as a team stronger than individuals working alone, but "the fist" also demonstrates that although each value is important, together, they unite a team to a common purpose.

When Coach K shows the Duke Blue Devils his fist, there is absolutely no question what message he is conveying. He has broken a complex message down into a very simple symbol that has been internalized in a way that the sight of the symbol inspires and motivates individuals to embrace and live out a common passion. "The Fist" is a symbol that says: "together we are stronger than one". The sight of it rallies the troops.

One of the greatest storytellers of all time, and perhaps a metaphorical genius is the former Head Football Coach of Notre Dame University, Lou Holtz. Dr. Powell conducted several interviews of former players to hear their perspective on his message to them as they worked toward team goals and objectives. During these interviews, one story emerged.

Coach Holtz emphasized "What's Important Now", encouraging his players to focus on the immediate critical "big rocks" that were today far more important than worrying about a National Championship several months down the road. "What's important **now**" dealt with the daily execution of becoming excellent. Becoming the best that we can be "today".

I was informed, "If we can be the best we can be every day, we can be better today than we were yesterday, and if every day we are better, every Saturday, we will put the best team we have ever had on the field". Learning to run, block and tackle better than anyone else built a framework toward excellence at Notre Dame University football.

"NOW". Coach Holtz focused on what is important "NOW". His metaphor was "NOW". According to players the word "NOW" was painted on the exit of the locker room that led onto the field, so every player was reminded daily that their objective was to think about dealing with the "NOW". When players return to the locker room, do you know what they see painted on the wall? "NOW". The message that Coach Holtz presented over and over was that dealing with the critical few things that are important

"NOW" (run, block, tackle, execution, grades, etc.) will result in their team's best results.

"WON", is "NOW" spelled backwards. "What's important "NOW"?

Metaphors are powerful. Brandon Podgorski, who has coached basketball at the Collegiate level as well as been an Athletic Director for nearly twenty years has used the phrase "Next Play" to articulate the message that no matter what happened a second or two ago does not matter right now, what matters now is now; the "next play". The dwelling on what just happened whether good or bad will distract you from the "next play". The next play is important.

How many times has celebrating a big play resulted in giving the opposing team an opportunity to score?

How many times has dwelling on making a mistake given the opposing team an opportunity to keep you from scoring, or kept you from doing something great?

Coach Podgorski explained it this way:

> No matter what happens during a game or practice, whether positive or negative (although it mostly came up after something negative happened), we would say "next play". It was a way to help them get over an error and get them back and focused on the task at hand.
>
> For example, a player would commit a turnover and I pull him out. I may have some constructive criticism for him at first but then it's always "next play". The turnover is done and over, let's move on and get ready for the next time you're out there.
>
> We also used it after something positive happened, especially after a big play. If a guy hit a big shot to put us up by one point but we still have five seconds left, I might call timeout and remind him, "next play". It was a great shot and be happy but let's move on and focus on getting a defensive stop.

It was a simple technique, but it worked. I'd even hear guys whispering it to themselves during practice when they needed a pick-me-up.

Legs Feed the Wildcat

The 1980 USA Olympic Hockey Team, in their victory over Russia en route to the gold medal, will forever be remembered as one of the greatest sports stories of all time. Sports Illustrated named it the number one sports moment of the 20th century and is known worldwide as the "Miracle on Ice". Herb Brooks was the legendary hockey coach who led the United States to defeat Russia at the 1980 Winter Olympics in Lake Placid, New York and then went on to win the gold medal. As a decided underdog in the Olympics, Coach Brooks would tell his players "the legs feed the wolf". His thought process in using this metaphor was knowing that Team USA may not have the most talented team on the ice, but his players would be the best conditioned.

The Daemen College NCAA women's triathlon team has adapted this metaphor from Herb Brooks to "the legs feed the Wildcat" because the Daemen College mascot is a Wildcat. These student-athletes know the importance of lower body strength and power. They understand that hard work is needed, and limits need to be pushed each and every day if they want to achieve their goals. They will need a balance of talent, skill, and effort. However, at the end of the race, it will be the superior condition student-athlete who has the mental and physical strength to carry them across the finish line ahead of the competition. Whether a Wolf or a Wildcat the metaphor is a strong one. The strength and the conditioning of their legs keep their appetite for success well fed.

Individual Exercise 5.2: Simplify Your Message

1. Finally, reflecting on the values/mission/vision/ purpose statement you wrote in Chapter 3. Begin to draft your final version. Simplify your message! As succinctly as possible (less than 20 words) rewrite your statement addressing how the 3-5 most unshakeable, non-debatable, and non-compromise-able values will be lived out in your life. This draft might be a work in progress but

should eventually be perfected to a statement that is memorized, internalized, and lived out.

_____

_____

_____

_____

2. Think of or develop a symbol, metaphor, phrase, or a picture that will articulate the importance of your statement and what it means to you. Be prepared to present it to your teammates and give your 30 second elevator speech.

_____

_____

_____

_____

Team Exercise 5.1: The Shield

1. As a team, accumulate your team's 3-5 most widely shared values. These are the values that individuals hold dear but are also shared by other individuals on your team.

_____

_____

_____

_____

_____

2. Based upon your team's 3-5 most widely shared values (from question 1 above), as a team, discuss a Value/Mission/Vision purpose statement like the individual statements you wrote in Chapter 3. You can follow the same steps if you need to in an attempt to refine your values and values statement. To finalize this statement, write down your statement addressing how your team's 3-5 most unshakable, indisputable, and most firmly rooted values will be lived out as a teammate to your team. This statement should be one, when completed, that the entire team will embrace and live out in practice.

_____

_____

_____

_____

_____

3. Finally, as a team, develop a symbol, metaphor, phrase, or picture...that will articulate the importance of your team's agreed-upon statement and what it means to your team. Be prepared to present this representation to the class and your team and give an accompanying 30 second elevator speech.

_____

_____

_____

_____

_____

Chapter 5 Notes

Section II
Creating a Culture of Trust and Mutual Responsibility

Chapter 6

The Importance of Trust

"The toughest thing about the power of trust is that it is very difficult to build and very easy to destroy."
— Thomas J. Watson

Trust in Family and Friends

You can probably think of time in your life when you have lost trust in someone, whether a teammate, coworker, family member or friend. A time when someone said they would do something, but didn't follow through, or said one thing but did another, or did not share the whole truth, or acted unethically. Most likely, this experience changed the way you thought of this person, changed your perception of who this person was, and quite possibly changed the entire relationship with him or her.

Trust in Sport Teams

When there is a breakdown in trust within a sport team, the resulting feelings, perceptions, and relational weakness have an amplified impact and a multiplying effect over a number of individuals.

For example, a breakdown in trust between two offensive linemen not only affects the relationship between the two linemen but impacts the relationship of the other ten offensive players as well. Consequently, this breakdown in trust affects the whole team performance, and the entire locker-room. This is an example of the athlete's trust in each other. Athletes must work together in team sports if the team is to be successful. Everyone on the team needs to trust that each player will perform to the best of their ability. In addition to the athletes' trust in each other, several other trust relationships exist within a team including athlete's trust in the coach,

coach's trust in the athletes, and athlete's self-trust. Athlete's trust in the coach is when the athletes must be able to trust that the coach will provide them with the appropriate knowledge and support to reach their potential. Coach's trust in the athletes recognizes that coaches need the ability to trust the athletes executing what they have been taught and practiced. Additionally, the coach must trust that each athlete is giving full mental and physical effort when called upon. Athletes' trust in each other is the relationship of athletes working together in team sports if the team is to be successful. Everyone on the team needs to trust that each player will perform to the best of their ability. Finally, is an athlete's self-trust or self-confidence to execute and perform at a level that will contribute to the success of the team.

Trust in Business

When one player jeopardizes the trust of another teammate, there is a cascading effect. This phenomenon exists in all types of organizations, not just athletic teams. Evidence shows that a breakdown in trust has devastating consequences in organizational performance.

In business, a breakdown in trust, results in a breakdown in the nexus of contracts between the various stakeholders that our capitalistic system is built upon.

Credibility and Trust are the foundations of leadership and have a profound impact on organizational performance. People need to believe in their leaders in order to willingly follow them into the unknown. Substantial research proves that throughout history, and especially today, there are two leading characteristics that constituents look for in their leaders: honesty and integrity.

Research has also proven that trust exceeds all other traits as a contributor to team performance including player and coaching talent.

Trust IS That Critical

One of the reasons trust is so impactful to performance, leadership, and the team environment is because it allows teammates to willingly commit their hearts and minds to a common purpose. Higher levels of trust actually intensify the commitment of constituents and team.

People have stronger commitment and work harder in trusting environments because those environments make people feel valued, motivated, enthusiastic, challenged, inspired, capable, supported, powerful, and respected. As a result, team members are more willing to suspend their questions, doubts, and personal motives and instead commit themselves wholly into the shared goals of the team. When this occurs, teammates feel proud to tell others they are part of your organization.

By creating sensitivity to shared organizational values, vision, and purpose, you have facilitated a bond that can lead to creating a taste of ownership and attachment that is very powerful, culminating in mutual responsibility to achieve their desired outcomes.

Trust is the bond that holds a team together. Trust is the product of belief in your peers and teammates, and their commitment to your common goals, and shared aspirations. It is the faith that your fellow team members will act, speak, and live in alignment with your shared values and organizational purpose. Trust is the emotional connection that causes extraordinary things to happen.

A Dysfunctional Team Lacks....

In his best-selling book Five Dysfunctions of a Team, Pat Lencioni (2002) identified five dysfunctions that lead to team failure. The very first of the five dysfunctions Lencioni outlines is "Absence of Trust". Without trust, a group cannot authentically engage with each other, consequently making it improbable to meet organizational objectives, and its shared purpose. "No quality or characteristic is more important than trust…Unfortunately there is probably no quality or characteristic that is as rare as trust, either" (Lencioni, 2005, p. 13).

So why is trust so rare? I believe trust is rare because it seems to mean different things to different people. Because people tend to define trust in different ways, the word is used very inconsistently. Therefore, organizations rarely develop healthy and functional norms around mutually honest and open, healthy relationships.

How Do You Define Trust?

Trust is a word that can be difficult to define. You cannot see it, touch it, smell it, or taste it, but its existence or lack of, is painfully evident in relationships. Dictionary.com defines trust as:

- "reliance on the integrity, strength, ability, surety, etc., of a person or thing"
- "to rely upon or place confidence in someone or something"
- "to permit to remain or go somewhere or to do something without fear of consequences"
- "the condition of one to whom something has been entrusted"
- "the obligation or responsibility imposed on a person in whom confidence or authority is placed" (Dictionary.com, 2015).

We believe trust is an expectation or belief that a teammate can rely on another team member's actions, words, and intentions toward his/her peers and the team. It involves the feeling that arises within a team that practices regular, honest, and cooperative behavior based on commonly shared values, norms, and a common purpose.

Trust in high performing teams exists because in these few but very special teams, teammates believe in and live out their shared purpose (Ch. 1), shared values (Ch. 2), **shared vision** (Ch. 3), and communicate (Ch. 5) openly and honestly with each other.

In section II of this book, we will cover several subjects that will aid your team in building the type of trusting community that is necessary for creating and maintaining a high performing organization.

Building this type of environment is not easy and it doesn't happen overnight. Just like many of the other topics we have covered, building, and maintaining a trusting environment takes deliberate effort, practice, and hard work. Making the commitment to build this type of community requires your team to build individual and collective credibility (Ch. 7), build healthy and proper relationships (Ch. 8), and have shared and mutual responsibility (Ch. 9).

If you want to accomplish extraordinary results, and have a wonderful experience that will make a difference in your life and in the lives of others, we argue that building a culture of trust and mutual responsibility is well worth the hard work.

"Nothing makes the team environment more meaningful and enjoyable than when your team experiences an unshakeable bond of trust. Cohesiveness comes from trust. Dedication to one another comes from trust. Your role as a team leader requires you to actively engage in building the bonds of trust" (Dobbs, 2009, p. 41).

Things that Build Bonds of Trust

- Honesty
- Integrity
- Sacrifice
- Positive Attitude
- Confidence
- Optimism
- Success
- Failure
- Spirit of Togetherness
- Appreciating Others
- Recognizing Others
- Tolerance of Individual Differences
- Open Communication
- Ethical and Moral Actions
- Empathy
- Following Team Rules
- Shared Goals
- Shared Purpose
- Shared Values
- **Shared Vision**

Things that Break Down Bonds of Trust

- Dishonesty
- Resentment
- Selfishness
- Negative Attitude
- Breaking Team Rules
- Forming Cliques and Rivalries
- Frustration
- Lack of Ethics
- Cheating
- Egotistical Attitudes
- Not Living in Alignment with Team Values, Vision or Mission.

Exercise 6.1: Building Trust

1. How easily do you build trust in other people? Use two examples to support your answer.

   _____

   _____

   _____

2. What has been your very best team experience? Explain the level of trust that existed during that experience.

   _____

   _____

   _____

3. Have you ever been involved in an organization in which the bonds of trust have broken down? Describe your experience. What could have changed the experience for the better?

   _____

   _____

   _____

4. What three things can you personally commit to doing today that will build bonds of trust in your organization, and in other areas of your life?

   _____

   _____

   _____

5. How do you believe these actions/activities will impact your team and your life?

   _____

   _____

   _____

6. Review the elements that build and break the bonds of trust. Select at least five from each of the lists and briefly describe how the elements either build trust or break down the bonds of trust in your team.

    _____

    _____

    _____

7. Schedule a team meeting. Discuss with your teammates how choices they make can either build or break bonds of trust. Discuss the thoughts from questions 5 and 6. What activities/actions will your team commit to today to build bonds of trust?

    _____

    _____

    _____

Chapter 6 Notes

Chapter 7

Credibility: Model the Way and Live Your Message

"Be a light not a judge;...be a model, not a critic."
— *Stephen Covey*

At the core of building a trustful organization, is building credibility as a leader. Credibility is essential to building trust. Trust is essential to effective communication, and effective communication is essential to exemplary leadership. As we have stated earlier in this book: "How can you believe the message if you can't believe the messenger?"

People are driven by something that gives them meaning and purpose, but people won't commit themselves to work harder or more effectively for just anyone. People vote for leadership with their energy, dedication, loyalty, talent, and actions. But people don't put forth their highest quality efforts when they don't believe in the interests of their leaders (Kouzes & Posner, 2011).

Since followers are the ones who dedicate their energy, loyalty, and talent to their team, and leaders. It is essential to build an organization around the type of leadership that will ignite passion and belief in the vision of the organization, by making a positive difference in people's lives.

Followers will vote to follow leaders who help them achieve what they didn't believe was possible. Followers will vote for leaders who bring out the best in them. This type of leader gives attention without seeking it. This type of leader makes others around them feel like they can make a difference in people's lives too. In other words, they are leaders who serve the interests of their followers before serving their own interests. This type of practice among leaders inspires loyalty and commitment and requires high levels of credibility.

Just as High Credibility Leaders have a very positive impact on organizational climate and team performance, Low Credibility Leaders have a very negative impact on morale and performance.

So Just What is Credibility?

Credibility is derived from the Latin root word credo, which literally means: "This I believe". True and honest credibility begins with **credo**, or a grounded and internalized understanding of what one believes. Your credo is the same thing as your **doctrine**, or **personal philosophy**.

A great example of credo or a creed in the Christian tradition is the Apostles' Creed. This is the statement and foundational belief of the Christian Church:

I believe in God the Father, Almighty, Maker of heaven and earth: And in Jesus Christ, his only begotten Son, our Lord: Who was conceived by the Holy Ghost, born of the Virgin Mary: Suffered under Pontius Pilate; was crucified, dead and buried: He descended into hell: The third day he rose again from the dead: He ascended into heaven, and sits at the right hand of God the Father Almighty: From thence he shall come to judge the quick and the dead: I believe in the Holy Ghost: I believe in the holy catholic church: the communion of saints: The forgiveness of sins: The resurrection of the body: And the life everlasting. Amen.

This is called the Apostles' Creed. Just as it is important for us as Christians to have a creed by which we formulate and live out our beliefs and shared collective values, so it is important for teams to have a creed stating the beliefs of the team. It would be a creed. This would be statements by which every teammate would refer to as they build, what they believe to be, their collective values. Every team member would work continuously towards living by their shared beliefs and their collective values.

In Chapter 3, you began work on your own creed, by defining your values, and developing your personal mission statement. This was the beginning work for your own doctrine, and personal philosophy. The work on this statement may not be complete yet, because this leadership journey is a work in progress, but as we continue to move along, We want us all to continue to reflect on our Personal Mission Statement until it is a true statement that reflects our values, what we believe, and is a testimony to how we live our lives.

To gain and maintain real credibility, your credo, doctrine, personal philosophy, or mission, cannot be just words written in your book, but must also be truly lived out in your life. If you say it, you must practice it to have credibility. You believe it, now others need to believe in you.

Creditworthy

Another word that is derived from the Latin root credo is the word "credit". Credit, as used in the world financial system, is measurement of trustworthiness. It is the confidence that a banker or a lender has in a purchaser's intentions and willingness to pay, entitling a person with the capacity to buy or borrow. Lenders will check your credit history and your credit score and make lending decisions by closely scrutinizing your history of honoring your past obligations. Establishing credit with a lender is the same as establishing credibility with a lender. In other words, the more credible you are as a borrower, the more creditworthy you are. Followers are just like loan officers; they do a credit check before they commit their hearts to a leader.

One of the quickest ways to build credibility within your team, and gain the trust of your teammates, is to set the example you want others to follow. In other words, Model the Way for your team. Don't just tell them what you want them to be; how you want them to act; and the values, vision, and purpose by which they would live and play. Show them through your own actions, by Living Your Message. "Be a light, not a judge;…be a model, not a critic" (Covey, 1991, p. 25).

Leadership is a Relationship

Remember from chapter 1, as we worked through the topic of leadership, and its definitions? We discussed that leadership is a relationship that involves influence. We also discussed that influence is not gained overnight. Influence grows as we demonstrate who we are over time as we connect with our teammates and build relationships with them. As an exemplary leader, you want to influence through a trustful relationship with your teammates. As an exemplary, Transformational Leader, the kind of influence you want to have on your team is only gained by Modeling the Way and Living Your Message.

More than just about anything, people want to believe in their leaders. People really understand actions better than they understand words. People want to trust their leaders and have confidence that their leaders will follow through on their commitments. No one wants to follow a leader that they cannot trust. Building that type of trust means that as a leader you will **do what you say you will do** (DWYSYWD). You will set the example for others to follow; you will practice what you preach; you will live your message. In other words, "walk the talk".

Exercise 7.1: Credibility

1. What does the word credibility mean to you?

   _____

   _____

   _____

2. Think about the most credible person you know. What does that person do that makes you think of him/her? How can you incorporate these things into your daily life?

   _____

   _____

   _____

3. Think about the values you have spent time defining. Think about the mission statement that you have written for yourself. How consistent have you been in the past, in living out your stated values? Are you "walking the talk"? Explain.

   _____

   _____

   _____

4. Can you think of a leader who set the example by personally living the organization's values? In what ways does the leader do this?

_____

_____

_____

5. Exemplary Transformational Leaders personify their values. What will you do in the future, to live out your mission, and personify your stated values? How about the team mission and values?

_____

_____

_____

6. Exemplary Transformational Leaders model the way, and teach others to personify, and live out the values of the team. What will you do in the future to model the way for your teammates (physically, mentally, emotionally, socially, and spiritually)?

    a.   Physically

_____

_____

_____

    b.   Mentally

_____

_____

_____

    c.   Emotionally

_____

_____

_____

    d.   Socially

_____

_____

_____

e. Spiritually

_____

_____

_____

Chapter 7 Notes

Chapter 8

Relationships

Team relationships are very special relationships, because the sum of a healthy team is more enriching and enjoys a more rewarding experience than any one of its members can achieve on their own. In other words: We are better together. When these mutually enriching and rewarding relationships are built upon a foundation of trust, and credibility, a respectful culture can emerge and will have a major influence on the willingness of teammates to make great sacrifices for the organization. When mutually rewarding relationships are built upon a foundation of trust and credibility, the team becomes far more open to the type of influence that is necessary for teams to create extraordinary change. When these mutually rewarding relationships are built upon a foundation of trust and credibility, the team enjoys the fruit of extraordinary personal and organizational results.

Exemplary results do not happen in isolation. "Developing relationships means creating meaningful connections. Emotionally intelligent leaders encourage opportunities for relationships to grow and develop" (Shankman, Allen, & Haber-Curran, 2015, p. 159). One of the leading scholars on the topic of leadership, Margaret Wheatley (2002) theorized, "relationships are all there is. Everything in the universe only exists because it is in relationship to everything else. Nothing exists in isolation. We have to stop pretending we are individuals that can go it alone" (p. 19). Each team member has a role; and each team member must understand that role and how that role fits into the good of the team; and each member must respect and value the roles and contributions of others, while together, they are working toward the organization's **shared vision**.

Mutual Emotional Bank Accounts

Steven Covey (1989) compared relationships to bank accounts by using the metaphor that is akin to keeping track of a mutual emotional bank account's deposits and withdrawals. Covey believed that we each have emotional mutual bank accounts with other individuals. When we do something of value for them, we allegorically make deposits into our mutual emotional bank account. However, when we ask them to do something for us in a demanding or unhealthy or unreasonable way; or when we do something that hurts our credibility or our mutual trust towards each other, we take withdrawals from our mutual emotional bank account.

Healthy, mutually rewarding relationships grow out of having a mutual emotional bank account that has a positive balance. When any one individual makes more withdrawals than they make deposits, then the emotional bank account becomes overdrawn. When the mutual emotional bank account is overdrawn, it causes a breaking down of the bonds of trust, credibility and mutual respect that every team needs. It has the potential of becoming the factor that causes enough damage to destroy the relationships within the team.

Team members or leader/follower relationships break down and fail to meet mutual expectations; the relationships tend to deteriorate because teammates are striving to become interdependent and therefore vulnerable to each other. Clearly, when these scenarios take place, one must conclude that the mutual emotional bank account is overdrawn.

High Performing Synergistic Teams

High performing, synergistic teams that could produce exceptional results must be built on relationships with a positive emotional bank account balance. Remember from our discussion about **leadership** in Chapter 1, the word **relationship** is one of the crucial ingredients for the effective leadership process to work. It is the same type of personal emotional connection achieving leadership that affects team performance. This type of personal emotional connection comes out of the interplay of values, vision, credibility, trust, integrity, consistency, and empathy. This type of personal emotional connection leads to high morale. This type of personal emotional connection results in mutual commitment to team members and high performance of the authentic team.

Human relationships play a fundamental role in shaping our psychological experiences. In sport and performance, researchers are beginning to recognize the significance of relationships with regards to the development of an array of contextual psychological responses, and it is becoming clear that the study of relationships in the context of human performance is worthy of attention.

Building Authentic Relationships

Being authentic means being genuine or is often referred to as "being real". Most of this book has dealt with self-discovery, emotional intelligence, and in the process understanding who you are, and living it out.

Being authentic means knowing what you stand for. This has led us to this point where with this better understanding of ourselves, and those around us, we will discuss building the kind of authentic relationships that drive extraordinary teams to superior performance.

What does it mean to become an authentic team? When your team intentionally and deliberately internalizes and practices the lessons learned through the first six chapters of this book; you begin the process of sharing the collective authenticity that builds authentic relationships. When your team deliberately and intentionally talks, acts, and lives in alignment with your values, and your purpose; then your team will collectively be walking the talk or living out loud. This type of climate (understanding and living in alignment unapologetically) is what it means to become an authentic team.

Authenticity is a complicated, time consuming and all-encompassing process guided by a **shared vision** and fueled by intentional behaviors. Indeed, authenticity is an ongoing, constantly evolving journey. It is not accomplished with a 100-yard dash mentality. It is more like running a 26-mile marathon mentality. So, it is not hard to understand why very few organizations (sports or business) ever compete at the highest levels; and it is not hard to understand why few organizations ever reach their full potential. Authenticity does not develop overnight; rather, as mentioned in earlier chapters, authenticity like leadership is an ongoing journey. If your team is willing to take the journey, you will clearly separate yourselves from the pack. A great deal of research and evidence suggests that the top 25% of emotionally intelligent organizations outperform the bottom 25% by over 400% (Goleman, Boyatzis, & McKee, 2002). Is there any wonder now why some sports and corporate organizations consistently outperform others year after year and season after season? They take the time and make the effort! They take all the necessary steps on this authentic journey.

Exercise 8.1

1. In your own words, what does authenticity mean to you?

   _____

   _____

   _____

2. Can you think of a metaphor for authenticity?

   _____

   _____

   _____

3. Describe who you are when you are authentic.

   _____

   _____

   _____

4. What obstacles get in the way of you being an authentic teammate (beliefs, self-images, attitudes, emotions)? Explain.

   _____

   _____

   _____

5. In what situations has your authenticity been compromised? Why do you think that was the case? What were the outcomes? Is there anything that you would do differently?

   _____

   _____

   _____

6. Schedule a team meeting. During this meeting discuss what individual and collective authenticity means for your team. What do you plan to do in the next 6 months to build stronger, more powerful relationships? What do you want your team to be like in one year from now as a result of this activity?

_____

_____

_____

7. Develop a monthly plan for measuring and improving your team performance in building appropriate authentic team relationships.

_____

_____

_____

Chapter 8 Notes

Chapter 9

Mutual Responsibility

Responsibility means acting in a manner that best serves the interests of yourself, family, organization, and team. Responsibility is the duty, the charge, or obligation to make decisions and follow through with them. Responsibility is about activities and issues that serve the interests of oneself, others, or the organization.

Mutual responsibility means that no one person is "in charge" and everyone must contribute. It means no single person has the best or right answer, so you must build broad commitment to action. It means that each person is expected to have a viewpoint, to surface conflicts and concerns, but also ensure that their views are relevant and compelling for others. And, most especially, it means having the conversations that most people avoid, and performing them with skill and grace. Mutual responsibility within a team is about the team, not about the individual members of the team and requires a sense of duty (Schlenker et al., 1994).

Taking personal responsibility involves aligning your actions and decisions with your authentic self's plan for the ideal future. Taking personal responsibility is about being disciplined to do things routinely and deliberately that move you closer to your vision for the ideal future. Taking personal responsibility is about being responsible for one's own wellbeing by taking intentional action to change.

Being healthy, wealthy, and wise seldom happens by accident. It typically takes place over a period of time. Being intentional about being healthy, wealthy and wise compels one to make intentional and principled decisions on a daily basis to take care of small things in a responsible manner that eventually leads to big improvements in personal circumstances.

Being responsible for taking care of yourself inside and out begins with an understanding of one's personal values, vision for their ideal future, and an internalized commitment to live in alignment with their personal mission or credo. This is why we spent so much time in chapters 1 through 4 of this book defining what is important to us and how we see our future.

> *"You cannot escape the responsibility of tomorrow by evading it today."*
> *—Abraham Lincoln*

Without a clear understanding of who we are, it is impossible to live in an authentic way. We must prioritize our high worth activities and be intentional about living by our personal values, our vision for our ideal future and our commitment to live within the parameters of our personal mission or credo.

Multiple global studies have reported evidence that shows that as little as 23% of our time is spent on important productive activities that lead toward accomplishing extraordinary results. The reasons cited for this phenomenon were really very simple. One reason is wholly a result of the lack of prioritizing activities around one's authentic self (Kogon, Merrill, & Rinne, 2015).

Another reason is spending valuable, precious time and energy on unimportant things that became urgent due to lack of taking responsibility up-front (Bodell, 2012). When we don't take responsibility for the little things today, they can become the urgent problems of tomorrow. Failing to focus on growing in the social, emotional, mental, and physical aspects of one's character and life impedes the mutual responsibility of the **team**.

Eating right, exercising, saving money, building proper relationships, becoming better educated, focusing on continuous improvement, and growing as a person are all critical responsibilities. You owe these critical responsibilities to any team you belong to today. You owe these critical responsibilities to any team you hope to belong to in the future.

Consider the Consequences

Your Professor requires you to complete all your assignments and show your rationale for your answers. However, your Coach expects you to be at practice on time (Coach's view of "on time" means 15 minutes early). Everyone is on your case to do the right thing; to **do what you say you will do** (DWYSYWD); to be responsible. But there is a lot more to being responsible than doing what other people want you to do. Being responsible means making the right choices. Being responsible means identifying and accepting the consequences – good and bad – of your decisions. Being responsible ultimately means considering how your actions will not only affect yourself, but the people and situations around you.

Five Essential Elements of Responsibility

1. Honesty – Honesty comes from the word honor, which means high respect, worth, merit, or rank. Honesty requires sincerity and fairness. The old saying really is true; "Honesty is the best policy". Some of the characteristics used to describe honest people are:
    *   Respects other people's property.
    *   Always tell the truth.
    *   Care passionately about others.
    *   Speak and act in alignment with beliefs.
    *   Admit when you are wrong.
    *   Have the strength to tell others when you believe they are wrong.
2. Compassion/Respect – Compassion and Respect requires a sense of esteem, mercy, and tenderness for the worth or excellence of another.
3. Fairness – Fairness requires being free from bias, dishonesty, or injustice. When you are fair, you treat others as you would want them to treat you. You apply impartiality, and you do not discriminate.

4. Accountability – Being accountable requires the willingness to be responsible, and answerable to someone, or for your actions. Accountability requires living in alignment or in a state of being responsible, answerable, and liable for your decisions, actions, self, and others.

5. Courage – Referred to as Bravery, Boldness, Fearlessness, Mettle – as in Determination, Spirit, Vigor and Guts, Fortitude, Perseverance. Courage requires the ability to confront uncertainty, hardship, and opposition, and doing what is right when it is the hardest thing to do. Fortitude is so important that it is one of the seven "Gifts of the Holy Spirit".

Sharing the Responsibility and Making it Mutual

As a leader of the future you have a responsibility to learn, grow, and change. Research has shown that it requires deliberate practice to improve mentally, physically, emotionally, socially, and spiritually. Sharing this responsibility with your team can lead to increased ownership, social responsibility, mutual trust, and credibility, binding obligations to achieve extraordinary results.

Mutual responsibility doesn't happen in a vacuum. It involves mutual trust, and mutual credibility. That is why we discussed these things in the previous chapters, but which comes first? Trust? Or does trust grow from individual and collective responsibility?

Mutual trust, and mutual credibility grows out of the collective individual expectations that arise within a community of regular, honest, and cooperative behaviors based on commonly shared norms.

When an organization and its norms are built on individual learning, growth, accountability, reliability, dependability, and the initiative to honor everyone's burden of obligation, the unit as a team, as a whole becomes capable of developing a mutually responsible climate.

Mutually responsible teams are bound by a social contract that whether written or unwritten, unifies and aligns actions and decisions on and off the field. This written or unwritten social contract aligns actions and decisions inside and outside of the boardroom. This written or unwritten social contract includes vision, mission, values, and the social obligation to accomplish the organization's shared purpose. When each and every team member strives to fulfil their individual and collective social duty, the collective team grows toward building a culture of mutual responsibility.

Exercise 9.1

In Chapter 1, we began our discussion about change, and concluded our chapter with team exercise 1.1 that addressed the five dimensions of personal change. In this exercise, each teammate should have reflected individually on factors that promote personal growth and change in each of the five dimensions in your individual lives. The next step was to reflect and list the factors or hurdles that hinder your growth and change within these factors. As a team, you should have followed these initial steps by discussing these same questions as a team, by asking "What were the factors that promote positive growth and positive change in each of the five dimensions?", "What are the obstacles that might seek to hinder us from promoting this positive growth and positive change?".

What we want you to do now is:

1. Revisit team exercise 1.1 and reflect once again on each of the Five Dimensions of Change.
2. As an individual, how will **you** commit yourself to achieve personal growth in each of the Five Dimensions?

    _____

    _____

    _____

3. As an individual, what will **you** commit yourself to that will work toward eliminating the factors that hinder positive change within each dimension?

    _____

    _____

    _____

4. In a separate document, we want you to write a statement about your commitment and responsibility to make these changes a reality in your life.
5. Personalize this document and sign it.

6. Hang this document in plain sight on your mirror where you can see it, as well as on your locker where your teammates can see it. You are making a commitment to them to exercise your responsibility as a team mate to grow in each of the Five Critical Dimensions of Change and Leadership.
7. Call a Team Meeting.
8. In this meeting discuss your personal statement with your team.
9. Finally, revisit as a team your previous outcomes from team 1.1. Has anything changed? Discuss how the team will grow and commit collectively to activities within each of the Five Dimensions. Remove all obstacles and hold yourself and the collective team **responsible** for following through on each of the Five Dimensions.

Chapter 9 Notes

Chapter 10

Continual Improvement

"Strive for continuous improvement, instead of perfection."
— Kim Collins

Asking the question; "As good as we are; how can we become better?" is about seeking ways to continually improve. Throughout this book, the related exercises, and workshop activities we have begun down the path of implementing a Continual Improvement Process (CIP). As you can see, beginning a CIP is time consuming, but easy. The difficult part of this time-consuming process is actually making it continual. The process of making Continual Improvement (CI) part of the DNA or genetic code of your team or organization requires committing to an ongoing practice of seeking to understand desired outcomes through reflection and the development of a values- driven vision. Continual Improvement is based on these three things:

- Feedback: The core principle of CIP is the (self) reflection of processes.
- Efficiency: The purpose of CIP is the identification, reduction, and elimination of suboptimal activities, practices and behaviors, and replacing them with correct and right activities, practices and behaviors.
- Evolution: The emphasis of CIP is on incremental, continual steps of growth and change rather than giant leaps.

CI is a philosophy that seeks to improve all the processes, activities, and behaviors related to a transformation process on an ongoing basis. In this philosophy, everyone - players, coaches, labor, and management are involved in identifying gaps in the current state of affairs and in the ideal future. In this philosophy of continuous improvement, the objects are centered on designing activities, practices, and behaviors to create intentional organizational growth and intentional change. This philosophy is concerned with taking personal and collective responsibility to continually challenge and improve ourselves as individuals, teammates, and professionals within and outside of our organization.

> *"Excellent firms don't believe in excellence — only in constant improvement and constant change."*
> — Tom Peters

CI permeates the Japanese culture and their word for continuous improvement. The Japanese term "kaizen" is often used interchangeably with the term "continuous improvement" in professional literature and training. From the Japanese character *kai*, meaning change, and the character *zen*, meaning good, taken literally, it means *good change*.

The driving force behind CI and kaizen is in dissatisfaction with the status quo. CI and kaizen are concerned with moving from your current state, to an ideal future state, no matter how good of an organization other organizations may think you are. Standing still will allow the competition to overtake and pass any complacent firm.

Problem solving is an essential mindset for continual improvement to be successful. Actually, for Continuous Improvement to become a reality it must become a way of life. Continuous Improvement must become a culture that is assimilated into the thinking of coaches, teammates, management, and workers alike. In other words, Continuous Improvement must become part of the genetic code and DNA of the organization.

Continuous Improvement must occur especially during the off season. teammates, and coaches should continuously spot obstacles that hinder or have the potential to hinder growth and improvement in the individual and organizational five dimensions of leadership, and in the process of achieving the organizational mission. When such obstacles do occur, it is important to remove them quickly, and spot opportunities to improve.

A culture of CI within Transformational organizations is one in which leadership is shared, and individuals are growing, learning, and contributing to the overall goal. Teammates, coaches, schools and administrators, management, workers, communities, and families all have the potential to foster continual improvement. Through ongoing communication, information sharing, assessments and celebration of each small win, individuals and teams can progress towards personal and organizational goals. Here are the steps for developing a culture of continuous improvement.

> *"Without continual growth and progress, such words as improvement, achievement, and success have no meaning."*
> — *Benjamin Franklin*

Steps to Developing a Culture of Continuous Improvement

Continuous Improvement is the on-going effort to improve overall individual and organizational performance on a day to day basis by making small, incremental improvements within an individual, team, or business. It is based on the belief that these incremental and specific changes will add up to major improvements over time, changing the culture of the organization to focus on opportunities for improvement rather than focusing on reacting to problems.

Here are four factors that are essential to successful continuous improvement programs:

1. Leadership that Walks the Talk (DWYSYWD)

    The support of an organization's leadership team is usually cited as the number one factor for the success of a continuous improvement initiative. Leaders must exhibit behaviors that not only demonstrate support for the initiative but also the behaviors that they wish all employees to emulate. This ultimately comes down to guidance and the support within the organization to make the change. If there is not adequate support for a continuous improvement program to be implemented, then the team charged with implementing it will be operating on what will be, in effect, a series of isolated efforts.

2. Focus on "Fire Prevention" not "Firefighting" (Be Proactive)

    Building a vision-driven, transformational organization that is built on shared values will allow coaches and teammates to focus on the important longer-range goals that drive an organization to its ideal future. Also, a vision-driven, transformational organization built on shared values will allow coaches and teammates to make daily incremental growth, improvement, and change possible.

    This type of culture will aid your organization in focusing on priorities that are proactive in reaching your long-range goals rather than reacting to the problems that seem urgent. No individual, coach, manager, worker, team, or company can implement incremental daily growth and change if they don't have the time or mental capacity to do so when they are constantly solving urgent problems or "firefighting".

    The trouble is that often it is the very seemingly urgent problems that need fixing that are creating a series of "fires" that constantly distract teammates and coaches from making daily incremental improvements.

    We spent considerable time in the first few chapters on individual and team discovery because proactive changes start on the inside and work their way to the outside. Transformative leaders understand that they control their own decisions about the activities that move them closer to their ideal future as opposed to outside circumstances or the urgent problems (fires) of today.

    The word responsibility can be broken down to *Response-Ability*, meaning that you have the *Ability* to choose your *Response*. Will you choose a proactive focus on daily growth and improvement or will you choose a reactive focus on putting out the fires of yesterday? It is about "fire prevention" rather than "firefighting".

3. Constancy of Purpose

Statistical scholar, and engineer, best known for his work in post WWII Japan, Dr. W. Edwards Deming formulated the "constancy of purpose for continual improvement". Constancy of purpose refers to the ceaseless commitment to continually asking ourselves both individually and as a team and organization, "As good as we are; how will we become better?" It is not good enough to have played your best game on Saturday or Sunday. What is necessary for a Continual Improvement culture to take hold and become part of your organization's culture and DNA is to proactively and relentlessly seek ways to be better today than yesterday and be better tomorrow than today.

When a Continual Improvement culture permeates everything an organization does, teams have the ability to bounce back from crushing defeats and avoid the letdowns that many teams experience following their biggest victories. The reason for this phenomenon is that the constancy of purpose is in daily and weekly continual improvement as opposed to short term highs and lows.

4. Mission Minded

When teammates, coaches, managers, and workers are focused solely on whether they're up for each week's game or meeting monthly or quarterly targets, it can become very difficult to prioritize improvements that will make a transformative impact over the longer term. Being Mission Minded allows you to focus on proactive decisions that will assist you in moving incrementally closer to your long-range goals and individual and **shared vision** for the organization as opposed to worrying about yesterday's urgent issues and problems, or today's distractions. Continual Improvement is as much a mind-set about being Values-Driven and Mission-Minded as it is about actions. In previous chapters of this book, your organization developed a **Shared Vision**, and Mission for your organization for the purpose of designing a Mission-Minded culture. The purpose of those earlier sections and associated exercises were to assist you as teammates, coaches, and organization in beginning the process of developing and seeing a picture of the ideal future for you and your organization, and to begin to focus on the longer-term.

This section of the book is intended to assist you and your organization in looking at, and considering the long-term impact of the work you do daily to continually learn, grow, and improve in order to make your **Shared Vision** a reality. It is important to understand that the results on the scoreboard each game is not as important as the continual improvement that moves you closer to your **Shared Vision**, and the continual improvement that places you in a better position to accomplish your long-range goals.

Chapter 10 Notes

Chapter 11

Sharpen the Saw

The Lumberjack Story

It was the annual lumberjack competition and the final was between an older experienced lumberjack and a younger, stronger lumberjack. The rule of the competition was quite simply who could fell the most trees in a day was the winner.

The younger lumberjack was full of enthusiasm and went off into the wood and set to work straight away. He worked all through the day and all through the night. As he worked, he could hear the older lumberjack working in another part of the forest. He felt more and more confident with every tree he felled that he would win.

At regular intervals throughout the day the noise of trees being felled coming from the other part of the forest would stop. The younger lumberjack took heart from this knowing that this meant the older lumberjack was taking a rest. He thought that meant he could use his superior youth and strength and stamina to keep going.

At the end of the competition the younger lumberjack felt confident he had won. He looked in front of him at the piles of felled trees that were the result of his superhuman effort.

At the medal ceremony, he stood on the podium confident and expecting to be awarded the prize of champion lumberjack. Next to him stood the older lumberjack who looked surprisingly less exhausted than he felt.

When the results were read out, he was devastated to hear that the older lumberjack had chopped down significantly more trees than he had, He turned to the older lumber jack and said, "How can this be? I heard you take a rest every hour and I worked continuously through the night. What is more? Old man, I am stronger and fitter than you". The older lumberjack simply turned to him and said: "Every hour I took a break to rest and sharpen my saw".

What is the Moral of the Lumberjack Story?

There are many messages that we can get from the lumberjack story. Perhaps on a shallow level we may see superficial meanings in the lumberjack story.

- A sharp saw is more effective.
- Why struggle with a blunt saw? Perhaps it is wise to take time to sharpen it.
- When we work more effectively, we get more done. Rest is just as important as hard work.

On a deeper level, we can see other meanings in the lumberjack story.

- Perhaps we should take notice that experience should never be underestimated.
- We can also take from this story that life and even a season is a marathon not a sprint.
- Rest is as important as work, and we should take time to plan and do things more effectively.
- The other message taken away from this story is one that has been made more familiar by Stephen Covey's 7th Habit of 'always sharpen your saw', where Covey sees the saw as a metaphor of the need to stay sharp in life (Covey, 1989).
- Likewise he discussed the need to continually 'look after your tools' (mental, social, spiritual, emotional, physical), and he used this story and this metaphor to emphasize the need to keep learning, improving, and engaged in self-renewal (Covey, 1989).

Referring to our previous chapter, we believe this fable makes a case to focus on the day to day things that help us improve continually in a way that moves us closer to our **Shared Vision** for the future. It is a metaphor that emphasizes the need to continually sharpen yourself and sharpen your team. It is a metaphor for organizing, on an on-going basis, in the critical domains in your life that make you most effective.

Sharpening the Saw is difficult to do when we are reactive and dealing with the urgent emergencies of the day. Have you ever made any of these comments?

- "I didn't have time to…",
- "I ran out of time because…", or
- "I had too many other things to do because…?"

Constantly dealing with the urgent situations that are presented every day and every week. For example: big assignments due tomorrow; presentations that are scheduled in the next day or two; final exams; a large order that needs to be processed immediately; can distract all of us from proactively working on the important things that make us extraordinary in the long-run.

Sharpening the Saw becomes a reality and a **proactive behavior** when it is not just a thought but a way of life. Making the concept of sharpening the saw a way of life takes a commitment to use our most important goals and values to plan our activities and make decisions about what we decide to work on in order to accomplish each day things that need our attention because they are an integral part of the bigger picture of our ideal future.

Planning these activities requires prioritizing what you will do to continually improve on a regular basis. We suggest that you prioritize weekly based on your long-range goals.

Once prioritized based on your previous exercises, we suggest using a weekly calendar where your continual improvement plans are scheduled in the same way that your other important meetings, classes, and assignments are scheduled.

Putting them on the calendar with other scheduled meetings gives them credibility and relevance. Yes, we recommend that you actually schedule in your calendar a time to reflect and meditate so you can develop spiritually.

We recommend that you actually schedule in your calendar a time to read to develop mentally. We recommend that you actually schedule a time to exercise to develop physically.

We recommend that you actually schedule a time to spend time with your family, friends and loved ones to develop socially.

And we recommend that you actually schedule a time of reflecting on your impassioned desire that is fed by your spiritual calling and become your ideal self.

As an example, though we recommend this sort of reflection and scheduling time on a weekly basis, as an IRONMAN® Triathlete, Dr. Powell scheduled his workout periods over a period of months while training, and input them into his digital calendar so he not only had it planned, but his staff, and colleagues also knew that it is a planned activity that happened from 4:00 AM until 7:00 AM every morning, and from 4:00 AM until 12:00 PM on Saturdays.

Daily reflection time and mental (reading and study) time should be scheduled. We schedule times for social activities, and we schedule time to plan for the future.

When all of these proactive initiatives are scheduled, they do not get jeopardized by urgent issues that will clamor for our immediate attention.

In fact, those urgent issues and problems have been greatly diminished and shortened by our commitment to planning and being proactive. Though emergencies do arise, and unforeseen problems do surface and we do address them. But because we have been proactive, and we have taken care of what we could and should take care of at the right time, the severity of and the urgency of problematic issues cease to hinder our plans. Scheduling the important proactive activities takes 90% of the urgency out of most potentially mind-bending situations.

We, as well as many of our clients, athletes, and students who have followed this recommendation have realized that they have found a lot more time in their schedules. At the same time, they have improved their performances, their grades, and their professional performance.

Mental Fitness

Just like an athlete needs to stay in peak athletic shape, a leader needs to be in great mental shape to maintain the leadership edge. This is about sharpening the saw to stay mentally fit. Maintaining and increasing mental fitness means having a keen awareness of relevant topics and information to grow your capacity as a leader. Most often people will stop learning once they are no longer engaged in formal education.

Earning a college degree, even a terminal degree, should not stop the learning process. Learning is a lifestyle and there is no finish line in the learning process. Great leaders are great because they intentionally continue to learn in various ways, such as:

- The great leaders **read books**. The best leaders make time to read every day and read four to five books each month.
- Leaders who want to improve **get training or coaching**. Every leader has room to become better at communicating, teaching, listening, or understanding.
- **Asking the right questions**, of the right person, at the right time, is how exceptional leaders learn to make the best decisions.
- The best leaders **listen well** and actively hear what is being said. Additionally, they continue digging by asking questions as noted above.
- Top leaders always **consider new ideas**. They are eager and curious to learn more and are open to what they do not know or understand.

To lead you must learn and constantly keep your saw sharp to achieve and maintain your mental fitness.

Exercise 11.1

Schedule time to "Sharpen the Saw"

1. If you use a regular calendar or regular scheduling system **great**! If you do not, find something that will work for you. You could use your computer, your phone, a paper-oriented calendar there are many options. The important thing is to find one that works for you. We personally use our smartphones that synchronize with Outlook on our computers so that we can see it wherever we are. This works best for us because family, faculty, and staff can always access it and know exactly what we are doing.

2. Recognize the things you are already doing regularly that are moving you toward improving in the five domains of leadership. To remind you, they are mental, social, spiritual, emotional, and physical. Schedule them in your calendar as appointments or recurring events even if you only have one or two of the five right now. You are probably already doing some of them. Put these times in your calendar so that they become solidified. Practice seeing them for about three weeks so as to make them a tangible part of walking your talk.

3. After 3 weeks of practicing, pick 1 or 2 additional domains of leadership that you want to focus on, and schedule them into your calendar. Try your best to work on these activities. Some of these activities can be scheduled for very short periods of time if you are not used to doing them. Even if they are only 15 minutes on a regular basis, they can make a big difference.

4. When you get to this point, begin to keep a journal about the things you are experiencing. Who are you, and who do you want to become? Reflect on critical incidents that happen in your day to day life. What is it that makes you happy? What is it that makes you sad? What is it that creates fear in your life? What has made you mad? This is all part of the continual journey of self-discovery and will assist you in becoming an extraordinary leader. It could be that you only begin with a sentence or two, however; try to build on this habit to make it the most meaningful for you as a practitioner of leadership.

Chapter 11 Notes

Chapter 12

The Team Life Cycle

As we have discussed throughout this book, transforming a group of individuals into a cohesive unit that can be described as a high performing team captivating deliberate practice, commitment to shared values, goals, aspirations, and a great deal of effort. Transforming a group of individuals into a cohesive unit takes a systematic approach to deliberate practice, deliberate observation & reflection, and deliberate learning by each individual teammate. It is the cumulative effects of this systematic individual learning that results in organizational learning or team learning.

In this chapter, we will outline the Team Life Cycle theory as developed by Bruce W. Tuckman (1965). Dr. Tuckman notes that all teams progress through a natural cycle made up of five stages on their journey from beginning as a disorganized group of individuals to an effective team.

Five Steps of the Team Life Cycle

The five steps of the team life cycle are:

1. Forming
2. Storming
3. Norming
4. Performing
5. Adjourning

We believe that when team leaders use Tuckman's principles of team dynamics, they are able to better provide the appropriate support to teammates and the team at the appropriate time. Let's outline the five stages and the characteristics of each stage.

Forming

Stage one of team development is forming. The team has just met, and all members are nice and pleasant to each other. The members of the team are eager to get started and to get to know each other. This stage is more focused on the people than the task of the team. Therefore, the team probably will not perform very well yet.

- Team members are uncertain about their roles and expectations
- Team members are assessing themselves and others to see where they fit
- In many cases teammates are pointed in different directions, and do not know what to expect
- Team members rely on strong, formal leadership
- Teams are directed by leaders at this stage
- Leaders in this stage must provide structure by assigning and clarifying tasks, roles, encouraging participation. It is critical that leaders encourage open and honest communication

Storming

Stage two is the storming stage. Here is when the task of the team becomes real and the members start to realize the weight and responsibility of successful task completion. This is when teammates stop being polite and start getting real. it is important to remember that most teams experience conflict and that disagreements are normal.

- Teams begin to take shape
- Individual personalities begin to show
- Teammates begin to struggle to assert their personal needs and goals while members challenge differences in an attempt to gain individuality and influence.
- At this stage teams lack the trust necessary to become cohesive
- Leaders in this stage must assist teammates to establish methods that support communication, encourage teammates to share honestly, and facilitate methods to resolve conflicts

Norming

Next is the norming stage. During this stage teammates begin to appreciate their team members' strengths and begin to settle in as a cohesive unit. The team may still experience conflicts. However, the conflicts occur less often and are resolved quicker.

- At this stage, the team is coming into its own, and the leader's standards are gaining acceptance
- Members are producing a cohesive unit
- Members themselves are setting standards about how they will work together
- Teammates feel more secure because the uncertainty and conflicts of the forming and storming stages are in the past
- Functional relationships are established
- Members are working collaboratively to accomplish shared aspirations
- Leaders facilitate and enable
- Leaders in this stage must talk openly and honestly about team issues. Encourage feedback. Continue to learn and encourage team learning and growth

Performing

In the performing stage, teammates are confident, motivated, and know what needs to be done with little or no direction. The team is focused like a laser and is moving in together on the final goal. This is obviously the stage for which all teams strive. Unfortunately, many teams do not make it this far because they cannot resolve conflict and fail at working together.

- Teammates have learned to work together
- Teams have aligned their actions and activities toward their shared values, mission, goals, and aspirations
- Teammates are committed to each other, the team, and the team goals

- Leaders at this stage can delegate and oversee this peer-led organization as it continues to strive toward the **shared vision** of the organization
- In this stage, it is critical that the teams jointly set goals are continually promoted and celebrated. Always celebrate small victories and learn from mistakes. Keep an ongoing assessment of the team and acknowledge each member's contributions. Develop every member to their fullest potential
- Celebrate, Celebrate, Celebrate

Adjourning

In 1977, a fifth stage called adjourning was added. At some point every team, even the great ones, must disband. This phase is difficult because teammates have become close, like family, and now feel at a loss because the experience has come to an end (Tuckman & Jensen, 1977).

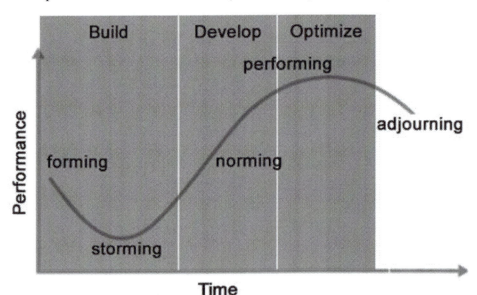

Figure 1 Timeline for forming a team.

Chapter 12 Notes

Works Cited

Ambrose, S. D. (2012). Who Cares? Pittsburgh, PA: Steel City Publishing.

Blanchard, K., Zigarmi, P., & Zigarmi, D. (2013). Leadership and the One Minute Manager. New York: Harper Collins.

Bodell, L. (2012). Kill the Company. Brookline, MA: Bibliomotion.

Burns, J. M. (1978). Leadership. New York: Harper & Row.

Choi, S.L., Goh, C.F., Adam, M.B.H. et al. Transformational Leadership, Empowerment, and Job Satisfaction: The Mediating Role of Employee Empowerment. Human Resource Health 14, 73 (2016).

Covey, S. (1989). The 7 Habits of Highly Effective People. Fireside: New York.

Covey, S. (1991). Principle Centered Leadership. New York: Fireside.

Crean, T. P. (2007). Coaching Team Basketball. New York: McGraw Hill.

Daft, R. L. (2005). The Leadership Experience (3rd ed.). Mason, OH: South-Western.

Dictionary.com. (2015, May 28). Dictionary.com. Retrieved from Dictionary.com: http://dictionary.reference.com/browse/trust?s=t

Dobbs, C. (2009). Becoming a Team Leader. Phoenix: Premier Graphics Publishing Group.

Goleman, D., Boyatzis, R., & McKee, A. (2002). Primal Leadership: Realizing the Power of Emotional Intelligence. Boston: Harvard Business School Publishing.

Hussain, S. T., Abbas, J., Lei, S., Jamal Haider, M., & Akram, T. (2017). Transactional Leadership and Organizational Creativity: Examining the Mediating Role of Knowledge Sharing Behavior. Cogent Business & Management, 4(1), 1361663.

Kennedy, John F. Inaugural Address. Washington, D.C. 20 January 1961. Speech.

Kennedy, John F. The Moon Speech. Rice University. Houston, TX. 12 September 1962. Speech.

King, Martin L. I Have a Dream. Washington, D.C. 28 August 1963. Speech.

Kogon, K., Merrill, A., & Rinne, L. (2015). The 5 Choices. New York: Simon & Schuster.

Kouzes, J., & Posner, B. (2007). The Leadership Challenge (4th ed.). San Francisco: Josse-Bass.

Kouzes, J., & Posner, B. (2008). The Student Leadership Challenge: Five Practices for Exemplary Leaders. San Francisco: Jossey-Bass.

Kouzes, J., & Posner, B. (2011). Credibility. San Francisco: Jossey-Bass.

Lencioni, P. (2002). Five Dysfunctions of a Team. San Francisco: Jose-Bass.

Lencioni, P. (2005). Overcoming the Five Dysfunctions of a Team. San Francisco: Jose-Bass.

Lewin, K., Lippitt, R., & White, R. K. (1939). Patterns of Aggressive Behavior in Experimentally Created Social Climates. Journal of Social Psychology, 10, 271–299.

Lincoln, Abraham. Gettysburg Address. Gettysburg, PA. 19 November 1863. Speech.

Lindsay, L. (2005). Ed.D. Organizational Leadership Conceptual Framework. Marion: Indiana Wesleyan University.

Maxwell, J. (1999). The 21 Indispensable Qualities of a Leader: Becoming the Person Others Will Want to Follow. Nashville: Thomas Nelson.

Hersey, P. & Blanchard, K. H. (1969). Management of Organizational Behavior – Utilizing Human Resources. New Jersey: Prentice Hall.

Powell, D. M. (2010). Transformational Leadership: its Effects On Job Satisfaction and Production Per Full-Time Equivalent In Autonomous Professional Organizations. Oakland City, IN: Oakland City University.

Schlenker, B. R., Britt, T. W., Pennington, J., Murphy, R., & Doherty, K. (1994). The triangle model of responsibility. Psychological Review, 101, 632–652.

Shankman, M. L., Allen, S., & Haber-Curran, P. (2015). Emotionally Intelligent Leadership: A Guide for Students. San Francisco: Jose-Bass.

Smith, M. L. (2001). Leading Change: In Your World. Marion: Triangle Publishing.

Tuckman, Bruce W. (1965) 'Developmental Sequence in Small Groups', Psychological Bulletin, 63, 384–399.

Tuckman, Bruce W., & Jensen, Mary Ann C. (1977) 'Stages of Small-Group Development Revisited', Group & Organization Studies, 2(4),419–427.

Werth, L., Markel, P., & Forster, J. (2006). The Role of Subjective Theories for Leadership Evaluation. European Journal of Work and Organizational Psychology, 15(1), 102-127.

Wheatley, M. (2002). Turning to One Another: Simple Conversations to Restore Hope to the Future. San Francisco: Berrett-Koehler.

Wooden, J. (1997). Wooden: A Lifetime of Observations and Reflections On and Off the Court. Chicago: Contemporary Books.

Appendix

Above and Beyond
Acceptance
Accessibility
Accomplishment
Accountability
Accuracy
Accurate
Achievement
Activity
Adaptability
Adventure
Adventurous
Affection
Affective
Aggressive
Agility
Aggressiveness
Alert
Alertness
Altruism
Ambition
Amusement
Anti-Bureaucratic
Anticipate
Anticipation
Anti-Corporate
Appreciation
Approachability
Approachable
Assertive
Assertiveness
Attention to Detail
Attentive
Attentiveness

Availability
Available
Awareness
Balance
Beauty
Being the Best
Belonging
Best
Best People
Bold
Boldness
Bravery
Brilliance
Brilliant
Calm
Calmness
Candor
Capability
Capable
Careful
Carefulness
Caring
Certainty
Challenge
Change
Character
Charity
Cheerful
Citizenship
Clean
Cleanliness
Clear
Clear-Minded
Clever

Clients
Collaboration
Comfort
Commitment
Common Sense
Communication
Community
Compassion
Competence
Competency
Competition
Competitive
Completion
Composure
Comprehensive
Concentration
Concern for
    Others
Confidence
Confidential
Confidentiality
Conformity
Connection
Consciousness
Consistency
Content
Contentment
Continuity
Continuous
    Improvement
Contribution
Control
Conviction
Cooperation

Coordination
Cordiality
Correct
Courage
Courtesy
Craftiness
Craftsmanship
Creation
Creative
Creativity
Credibility
Cunning
Curiosity
Customer Focus
Customer
  Satisfaction
Customer Service
Customers
Daring
Decency
Decisive
Decisiveness
Dedication
Delight
Democratic
Dependability
Depth
Determination
Determined
Development
Devotion
Devout
Different
Differentiation
Dignity
Diligence

Direct
Directness
Discipline
Discovery
Discretion
Diversity
Dominance
Down-to-Earth
Dreaming
Drive
Duty
Eagerness
Ease of Use
Economy
Education
Effective
Effectiveness
Efficiency
Efficient
Elegance
Empathy
Employees
Empower
Empowering
Encouragement
Endurance
Energy
Engagement
Enjoyment
Entertainment
Enthusiasm
Entrepreneurship
Environment
Equality
Equitable
Ethical

Exceed
Expectations
Excellence
Excitement
Exciting
Exhilarating
Exuberance
Experience
Expertise
Exploration
Explore
Expressive
Extrovert
Fairness
Faith
Faithfulness
Family
Family
  Atmosphere
Famous
Fashion
Fast
Fearless
Ferocious
Fidelity
Fierce
Firm
Fitness
Flair
Flexibility
Flexible
Fluency
Focus
Focus on Future
Foresight
Formal

Fortitude	Hygiene	Liberty
Freedom	Imagination	Listening
Fresh	Impact	Lively
Fresh Ideas	Impartial	Local
Friendly	Impious	Logic
Friendship	Improvement	Longevity
Frugality	Independence	Love
Fun	Individuality	Loyalty
Generosity	Industry	Mastery
Genius	Informal	Maturity
Giving	Innovation	Maximizing
Global	Innovative	Maximum
Goodness	Inquisitive	Utilization
Goodwill	Insight	Meaning
Gratitude	Insightful	Meekness
Great	Inspiration	Mellow
Greatness	Integrity	Members
Growth	Intelligence	Merit
Guidance	Intensity	Meritocracy
Happiness	International	Meticulous
Hard Work	Intuition	Mindful
Harmony	Intuitive	Moderation
Health	Invention	Modesty
Heart	Investing	Motivation
Helpful	Investment	Mystery
Heroism	Inviting	Neatness
History	Irreverence	Nerve
Holiness	Irreverent	No Bureaucracy
Honesty	Joy	Obedience
Honor	Justice	Open
Hope	Kindness	Open-Minded
Hopeful	Knowledge	Openness
Hospitality	Leadership	Optimism
Humble	Learning	Order
Humility	Legal	Organization
Humor	Level-Headed	Original

Originality
Outrageous
Partnership
Passion
Patience
Patient-Centered
Patient-Focused
Patients
Patient-Satisfaction
Patriotism
Peace
People
Perception
Perceptive
Perfection
Performance
Perseverance
Persistence
Personal
   Development
Personal Growth
Persuasive
Philanthropy
Play
Playfulness
Pleasantness
Poise
Polish
Popularity
Positive
Potency
Potential
Power
Powerful
Practical
Pragmatic

Precise
Precision
Prepared
Preservation
Pride
Privacy
Proactive
Proactively
Productivity
Profane
Professionalism
Profitability
Profits
Progress
Prosperity
Prudence
Punctuality
Purity
Pursue
Pursuit
Quality
Quality of Work
Rational
Real
Realistic
Reason
Recognition
Recreation
Refined
Reflection
Relationships
Relaxation
Reliability
Reliable
Resilience
Resolute

Resolution
Resolve
Resourceful
Resourcefulness
Respect
Respect for Others
Respect for the
   Individual
Responsibility
Responsiveness
Rest
Restraint
Results
Results-Oriented
Reverence
Rigor
Risk
Risk Taking
Rule of Law
Sacrifice
Safety
Sanitary
Satisfaction
Security
Self Awareness
Self Motivation
Self Responsibility
Self-Control
Self-Directed
Selfless
Self-Reliance
Sense of Humor
Sensitivity
Serenity
Serious
Service

Shared Prosperity
Sharing
Shrewd
Significance
Silence
Silliness
Simplicity
Sincerity
Skill
Skillfulness
Smart
Solitude
Speed
Spirit
Spirituality
Spontaneous
Stability
Standardization
Status
Stealth
Stewardship
Strength
Structure
Succeed
Success
Support
Surprise
Sustainability
Sympathy
Synergy
Systemization
Talent
Teamwork
Temperance
Thankful
Thorough

Thoughtful
Timeliness
Timely
Tolerance
Tough
Toughness
Traditional
Training
Tranquility
Transparency
Trust
Trustworthy
Truth
Understanding
Unflappable
Unique
Uniqueness
Unity
Universal
Useful
Utility
Valor
Value
Value Creation
Variety
Victorious
Victory
Vigor
Virtue
Vision
Vital
Vitality
Warmth
Watchful
Watchfulness
Wealth

Welcoming
Willfulness
Winning
Wisdom
Wonder
Worldwide
Work/Life Balance

Made in United States
Orlando, FL
13 July 2022